To Eileen and Paul

David Carlson

HAVING EVERYTHING:
A Father's Gift

Living Simply and Gratefully
in An Age of Acquisition

DANIEL J. CARLSON

WESTBOW®
PRESS
A DIVISION OF THOMAS NELSON
& ZONDERVAN

WestBow Press books may be ordered through booksellers or by contacting:

WestBow Press
A Division of Thomas Nelson & Zondervan
1663 Liberty Drive
Bloomington, IN 47403
www.westbowpress.com
1 (866) 928-1240

ISBN: 978-1-4908-6748-9 (sc)
ISBN: 978-1-4908-6749-6 (hc)
ISBN: 978-1-4908-6747-2 (e)

Library of Congress Control Number: 2015901111

Printed in the United States of America.

WestBow Press rev. date: 02/03/2015

Dedicated to
and in memory of
my mother,
Ruby Irene (Haskell) Carlson,
1908–2002,
whose partnership with my father
in marriage
immeasurably enhanced
both their lives.

Contents

Foreword

John W. Vannorsdall

This is a book sprung from gratitude. I haven't read about gratitude for a long time. I began this book with the assumption that it would be about World War I or the Great Depression of the 1930s. The author's father was born in 1897, as was mine, and for older people with such roots it's hard not to write about pennies and bullets. It turned out, however, to be a book about the profound gratitude of the author for the life of his father, J. Chandler Carlson.

At the least, one would expect a book set in the Depression and war years to provide us with the kinds of statistics that marked poverty and war. Those were the years when boys in school received, hopefully, one new pair of pants per year and grandmothers made a dress for the daughter. It may, at first, seem strange, but this book is not exploding with figures. It's about gratitude.

With a name like J. Chandler Carlson, I would expect that at least this chief character would be a well-tailored, well-educated, four o'clock cocktail type. It turns out to be the opposite. Chandler Carlson wears the white cover of a hospital orderly, is a member of a Swedish immigrant family, and his formal education ended at the sixth grade. He doesn't drink at all.

What is there to write and read about? This is a true and well-written story of a community of people whose way of understanding themselves was shaped by the law of God and by the compassion of

Jesus Christ. It was a small family shaped by a larger community where prayers were said and hymns sung and where those in need were served.

This is a book in which a son's gratitude for his father is shared with us. Our thanks to Daniel Carlson.

The Rev. Dr. John W. Vannorsdall served as president of the Lutheran Theological Seminary at Philadelphia until his retirement in 1990. He is a published author, served as the Yale University chaplain, in the chaplaincies of Cornell University and Gettysburg College and as a pastor of two congregations. From 1976 to 1990 he was the preacher on the Lutheran Series of radio's The Protestant Hour.

Preface

As the writing of this book neared its completion, the writer discovered that, without knowing it, he had heeded advice earlier given by C. S. Lewis, namely, advice given in "To a Schoolgirl in America," dated December 14, 1959. From a list of eight items of advice on writing, #6: "When you give up a bit of work don't (unless it is hopelessly bad) throw it away. Put it in a drawer. It may come in useful later. Much of my best work, or what I think my best, is the re-writing of things begun and abandoned years earlier."[1]

The remembrances and testimony that follow were begun in the fall of 1994, laid aside in 2000, and then not taken up again until the fall of 2013. Be it in the category of best work or otherwise, the ensuing pages have been both a joy and a privilege to write.

Jamestown, New York, gave several prominent personalities to the national and global communities in the twentieth century, including the late Robert H. Jackson, Associate Justice of the Supreme Court and the chief US prosecutor at the Nuremburg Trials; the late Lucille Ball, comedienne par excellence of TV's earliest days; and the late Roger Tory Peterson, widely acknowledged as the twentieth century's foremost ornithologist. Also noteworthy and close to both the writer's and the subject's heart, the four Lutheran congregations in Jamestown plus several congregations in adjacent communities, all of Swedish heritage, have over the past 100 to 130 years raised up in excess of sixty men and women ordained into the Holy Office of the Word and Sacraments.

Among such luminaries and preachers the name J. Chandler Carlson knows no such prominence, except to his contemporaries in Jamestown at midcentury whose lives he touched. While the locus of his influence was the hospital in which he worked for thirty-six years—addressed specifically in Chapter 16—each chapter highlights in some way the character and spirit of the man who came to be known to so many and whose simple lifestyle and overall humility nurtured each other.

Acknowledgments

This modest witness to a simple yet profound life would not have been possible were it not, first of all, for my wife, Faith, whose encouragement and assistance assured the transfer of the heart's and mind's treasure to the printed page. I am grateful also to my son, Curtis Carlson Russet, for the painstaking effort that went into the sketches that enhance nine of the chapters, and to my daughter, Carolyn Faith Carlson, whose maturity did not hinder the plain and, at points, childlike recollections of Epilogue II.

Also to be thanked are Betty Roxborough and Adeline Christofferson, a cousin and aunt respectively on my father's side of the family, as well as Thomas Oberg and Elaine Oberg Mattson, cousins on my mother's side of the family; Down East organic farmer and author, Cynthia Thayer; hometown friend, teacher, and author, Thomas A. Erlandson; hometown friend, former editor, and colleague, Ronald B. Bagnall; neighborhood friend and initial computer consultant, Alex George Bejan; friend, later computer consultant, and colleague, Nathaniel S. Anderson; the Rev. Daniel K. Nagle, pastor, and active lay member, Marcia Rupp, First Lutheran Church, Jamestown, New York; New England friend and retired professor of Accounting, Robert C. Waehler; briefly a New Englander but at heart and long since a Minnesotan and enthusiastic Chevrolet sales and leasing consultant, Matt E. Pagelkopf; a son of my internship supervisor and the one who clued me in regarding Singularity, Eric Inbody; Linda at Holy Trinity Lutheran Church, Buffalo, New York, as well as Sue at Niagara Falls

Tourism, Niagara Falls, Canada; to each and all of the following who reviewed the writing as it neared completion and whose comments were equally honest and encouraging: Richard Brakenwagen, Betty Combs, Sandy Ferria, Beth Groleau, Judy Jacobs, Carol Lundgren, Laurie Pavlos, Pam Pearson, James Peterson, Stephanie Roberts, and Paul Steinbrenner, whose question suggested the subject of Chapter 1; and friend and colleague, John W. Vannorsdall, whose early comments on my work encouraged me to persevere.

The photograph (July 29, 1961) included in Chapter 16 is provided courtesy of *The Post-Journal*, Jamestown, New York.

Introduction

"Simplify, simplify,"[2] was Henry David Thoreau's advice to his contemporaries. The following chapters are of a man whose life was typical for *his* time. Born at the end of Thoreau's century, his life was difficult in several ways. Mostly, it was simple.

Born on February 4, 1897, J. Chandler Carlson lived his entire ninety-two years, six months, and seventeen days in Jamestown, New York, at mid-twentieth century a thriving industrial city located in the southwestern corner of New York State.[3] Born to Swedish immigrant parents and the oldest of eight children, he remained at home close to half his life before marrying. His formal education ended in the sixth grade, and that was followed by a variety of jobs, including delivering groceries by horse and wagon, and later working with his father and two of his brothers in the sheet metal business. Yet it was as an orderly at the Jamestown General Hospital,[4] a job he began on a full-time basis in 1930 and that ended with his retirement thirty-six years later, that he became as well-known in the city of, at its peak and including several adjacent communities, some 50,000 people, as were most of the physicians whose orders he helped to carry out.

A recent fortune cookie prediction recalls a humorous incident while also highlighting my father's great strength. In the 1970s when he and Mom were visiting our family in Connecticut, we ate at a Polynesian restaurant in the greater Hartford area. At the meal's conclusion, we compared what each fortune cookie revealed, whether prophecy or wisdom—each of us, that is, except Dad. He claimed not to have received one, the rest of us concluding he had eaten it.

As for his great strength, the recent fortune cookie prediction states: "You will be of good comfort." That perfectly describes who my dad was, what he did, and how he is remembered.

Complexity seems to dominate life as the twenty-first century begins, and many of us would welcome a healthful dose of simplicity. Perhaps it is possible to simplify, not just because of current economic uncertainty, but also because it is best. Dad did not have a lot by the standards of an increasingly consumption-based culture. But in his view, he had not only all that was necessary; he had everything.

CHAPTER 1

---·•·---

What's in a Name, Really?

Afriend recently inquired about the second of my father's given names, that of Chandler. Considering his predominantly Swedish heritage, why an English name? It's a question I have only now begun to ponder seriously.

Might the name chosen have something to do with nineteenth-century immigrants wanting to identify themselves quickly as truly American—as in the given name being other than Nordic? Another possible influence was that in nearby Warren Country, Pennsylvania, there was a community named Chandler's Valley. And as noted in an ensuing chapter, the church to which the Carlson family belonged was, and remains, on Chandler Street. I never heard my grandparents explain why their first child was named Chandler. Nor did I ask.

My paternal grandfather, John Carlson, did not enter the country with the Carlson surname. A wooden trunk that accompanied him on the boat to what would become his new homeland sits in my home office, and still barely visible on its lid in white paint is the name *Nelson.* Unlike so many immigrants whose surnames were altered either intentionally or by mishap in the flurry of entrance happenings on Ellis Island, Nelson became Carlson once John was settled. Early in his American experience, he resided in a house that was home also to another John Nelson. Once too often having their mail mistakenly delivered, my future grandfather, while maintaining his Swedish identity, registered the new surname. So the sequence has been relayed from one generation to the next. But was it an entirely new name? My cousin, Betty, who has visited the family graveyard in Veigne, Sweden, says that some of the gravestones display both the names Nilsson and Karlsson. Whatever the case, from the anglicized Nelson to Carlson is hardly in itself a huge jump toward Americanization.

Some ten decades later, when John's great-grandson, Curtis Carlson, and his bride chose to take a new surname—rather than, as by then had become the practice of some, hyphenating their original surnames—Curtis' paternal grandmother's response surprised me. Dad had died five years earlier, but I insisted that Mom personally be told by Curtis himself that the family name of fifty-seven years was to be changed. Visiting Mom in Jamestown on a weekend, Curtis and Beth, over Sunday dinner and soon to depart for New England, had yet to raise the name change subject when the eighty-six-year-old grandmother asked, "Now, when I write to you young people, may I address the envelope Mr. and Mrs. Curtis Carlson?" To which her grandson replied, "Funny you should ask, Grandma."

Given Mom's age and the manner in which she was accustomed to addressing envelopes, that she asked the question at all seems strange. But if what Curtis then shared with her was expected to elicit a negative or shocked reaction, Mom's words were memorable. She began by saying, "You know, when I was a young woman, I often wondered why it was always the woman who had to change her name." Then, upon hearing the name that had been chosen, she continued: "When I was a child growing up on Bush Street, there was an orchard adjacent to our property. I've never eaten much fruit, but there was one tree the apple of which I liked, and that was the Russet apple."

The young couple had announced that the new surname was to be Russet, a name chosen because of its relation to nature. It soon became evident, too, that the lifestyle they would be sharing on coastal Down East Maine to a large extent reflected the name's archaic adjectival meaning, one related to simplicity. Little wonder that when they stopped for a visit in western Massachusetts on their return trip to Boston, Beth's first words upon entering the house were, "She's a great lady!" Indeed, Mom was a great lady, and not least of all as shown by her acceptance of what for some of her generation would have been a troubling, if not unacceptable, announcement from the younger generation. And adding to the mix on that wintry day in 1995 was the name of the restaurant where the young couple and the receptive grandmother had enjoyed dinner; namely, the Apple Inn. Surprisingly, in my mother's brief-entries diary on January 22, 1995, there's no mention of the announced surname change.

What's in a name, really? Plenty, and certainly an individual family's history, albeit a relatively small matter compared to a variety of current global issues, is often symbolized by the name itself. Given names, too, are not without significance. For example, Daniel, the first of this writer's given names, traditionally is understood to mean *God is my judge.* I don't recall either of my parents much stressing that meaning. Although I have been known to say that I may have been named Daniel Joseph for reasons of potential behavior modification— Daniel, according to biblical story, having once been in the company of lions, and Joseph having been sold by jealous brothers. The truth, however, is that I am so named because of the ultimate witness given by the two Hebrew notables, each one a person of faith, and that Daniel in particular was chosen because of a Bible study on the book of Daniel in which my mother had earlier participated.

All of which suggests the importance of character in a person's life and of how character, good or bad, influences the mere mention of a person's name and how it is heard. Read or hear the names Hitler, Stalin, or Idi Amin of the immediate past century, compared to Gandhi, King, or Mother Teresa, and very different sets of thoughts and images come to mind. The place in history of the first three is and will remain so very different from that of the second three.

What's in a name, *really?* Again, plenty. As already implied in the

Preface, the name Chandler Carlson isn't recognizable in any kind of universal sense. But to those who did know him, the name Chandler connoted much if not everything about the man described in the following chapters. As often as not, is it not primarily the *actions* of an individual that define who that person is? Hearing the name, even just the given name, recalls or suggests the actions. In my father's case, it's significant, too, that what the name Chandler, of Middle English and Old French origins going back five hundred years or more, means is *candle maker and seller.*[5] The reference, especially to candle, is an entirely appropriate reflection of how my dad, not least of all in his work, often came across to people—as a warm, glowing presence.

A name, in and of itself, communicates more about a person than often is realized.

CHAPTER 2

———◆◆◆———

Marriage: From Pickup Truck to No Car at All

It is difficult for children, especially young children, to imagine their parents being or doing many things. It is difficult imagining them ever having been children themselves. It is difficult imagining them ever not being present. By the time one begins to understand more fully the essentials of the human reproductive process, it is difficult to imagine one's parents making love. I suspect that, in spite of the mid-twentieth century sexual revolution, this pretty much remains true of today's pubescent youth.

It is difficult for me, even now, to imagine my dad, a confirmed bachelor in his late thirties, ever mustering the courage to ask for a date, let alone the determination to pursue a courtship. An old photograph shows him to be rather stern of face, with a hairstyle acceptable to the military, and wearing a pair of black-rimmed eyeglasses, none of which was uncommon for the day. Yet the one on whom his sights were set as a potential partner in marriage recognized that more stylish eyeglass frames would be both to Dad's benefit and to her liking.

But it was his relative lack of aggressiveness that causes me to imagine Dad as something less than a social charmer even in his early adulthood. How then, by the time he was in his late thirties—presumably firmly entrenched in bachelorhood's idiosyncrasies—did he find it within himself to take even the initial steps into a new life?

An equally compelling question is, what attracted Dad to Mom? Mom herself was an attractive young woman. Dad himself was not unattractive, but as I heard it from her, early on she felt sorry for him. That's the way she stated it. What Dad did or did not project to the young women Mom's age, I have no idea. But at a church picnic, as the eligible females apparently were sizing up eligible males in attendance, one said to another, "You can have Chandler." Surely the marriage from which I was soon to be born was sparked by more than these few lines convey.

As I learned fairly early in life, Dad had not been my mother's first love. In fact, she had been in love soon after graduating from high school—in love with a young man one year older than she, a man whose name was Matthew M. Hoff and whom she had met at her first job. Their relationship was serious enough so that, when I had reached midlife and was home for a visit, Mom one day asked me to drive down a street on the edge of town for the purpose of pointing out the house Matthew had built for when they would marry.

However, their relationship ended when, while twenty-three-year-old Matthew was in Chicago where he was both working and attending trade school, he tragically died, the result of a diving accident. It was July of 1930; Mom was twenty-two-years old and, as she revealed in her handwritten legacy notes at age eighty-four, "Oh, what a blow to my young life!"

Very recently I located a descendant of Matthew M. Hoff, the descendant's name being Matthew J. Hoff. The latter Matthew has resided all his life in Jamestown, New York, the same city to which his ancestor had moved before temporarily going to Chicago. I can't help but wonder what my mother might be thinking were she to be aware of this development—her son, nearly nine decades following the tragedy in Chicago, speaking with a descendant of the Matthew Hoff known to her, a descendant of the same given and surnames.

Had Matthew M. Hoff lived, would he and Ruby have married? Matthew was raised a Roman Catholic, and although Mom also wrote, "(His father) didn't know his son was going to go with me to my church," for many years the crucifix that lay atop the son's coffin hung in our home. It's significant too that my parents—Mom especially— were very unsettled when, in my senior year of high school, I briefly had a crush on a Roman Catholic girl. Of course, in part their reaction was indicative of not unusual pre-Vatican II relationships between Roman Catholics and Lutherans.

One thing seems certain: Had there been a Matthew and Ruby Hoff, these words would not have been written.

With that as background, my father's history was very different. Yes, according to Mom, he'd had a brief dating relationship with a young woman who, in fact, had been confirmed with my mother, but whose father felt that his daughter deserved someone better. And thus, on May 30, 1937, a Sunday and the day Dad and Mom married, my paternal grandmother said to her eldest child in her lilting Swedish brogue, "Well, Chandler, you've gone and done something we never thought you'd do!"

It was a small, intimate wedding, held before the immense altar of Jamestown's cathedrallike First Lutheran Church, and each one of the few immediate family members who was present must still have been so surprised by the exchange of vows that they were witnessing that no one thought to take pictures. Nor were any formal pictures taken beforehand or afterward. Today, only lifeless documents attest to the event having taken place.

Was there a honeymoon? There was, although a brief one to be sure—probably at most lasting only two or three days, as Dad would have had to take vacation days. It wasn't until the latter years of my childhood that his vacation time was increased from one to two weeks. The honeymoon location was some ten miles from home, on Chautauqua Lake just below the village of Bemus Point, where

Mom's parents owned a one-room cottage. In the winter it served as a storage space for their inboard motor boat in which my grandpa trolled for muskellunge. Come spring it was converted to a simple but comfortable living space. I recall Mom saying that neighbors across the street from the cottage were aware of the wedding earlier in the day and, in some manner, surprised the newlyweds during the evening hours. Considering the times and the story that here begins to unfold, the honeymoon site was, in its simplicity, appropriately symbolic.

Dad married, in part, outside his ethnic background. At the time, Jamestown was a dominantly Swedish community, but Mom's maiden name was Haskell. While her maternal Nording side was of Swedish heritage, her father's ancestors had migrated from Massachusetts to western New York—via oxcart, family lore has it—sometime in the nineteenth century. As a child attending public school, Ruby Haskell was often shy about her surname because it distinguished her from the majority of students in class. However, eventually she would outgrow that name-prompted embarrassment and, in my own maturity, I have been grateful for the blended blood in my veins. It keeps me mindful of the increasingly diverse American mosaic of which my family and I are but particles.

Ironically, when it came to diet, Grandpa Haskell was more Nordic than was his new son-in-law. Whether he was fed too much of it when being raised in the Carlson household or simply because he never did like it, as an adult Dad wouldn't eat things such as pickled herring or the highly odoriferous lutfisk. Both were, and for many continue to be, considered Swedish delicacies, especially at holiday time such as at Christmas. But Grandpa Haskell enjoyed both. "Some Swede you are!" Archie would chide Chandler.

Dad would say repeatedly over the years that he owed everything he had to Mom. Considering that when he courted her he did so in a pickup truck and that throughout their marriage they had no car,[6] what did he mean by *everything*?

He meant that had Mom not been the controller of the meager amount he earned working for the city—the Jamestown General

Hospital was city-owned—he may well have eventually ended his days alone, possibly destitute, and finally dying in a downtown tenement. At least that was Mom's occasional conjecture. It wasn't that Dad lacked the know-how needed to manage his personal responsibilities as much as it was that his spirit of generosity would have made him vulnerable to anyone intent on taking advantage of that spirit. Indeed, his lone surviving sibling and the youngest of the eight Carlson children, my Aunt Adeline Christofferson, now one hundred years of age, writes of her brother, "He had a heart of gold—not a selfish bone in him."

Fortunately for Dad and for us as a family, Mom was exactly such a controller, having brought a brief career as a bookkeeper in a local factory into their marriage. She kept family financial records as though their—and later our—lives depended on it. And in a sense they did. Dad and Mom together were generous, but always with their responsibilities to themselves also in view. Still, it's a fact that there was never a car, because Dad's income all his working years would not support that luxury. We got where we needed to go by walking, by public transportation, and often with the thoughtful assistance of extended family and friends.

It's also a fact that Mom and Dad—with Dad's dominant Swedish background and Mom's Swedish background on the maternal side—consistently chose not coffee but tea as their beverage of choice during the evening meal. Which of the two, Mom or Dad, initially suggested that choice, and why? Was it driven by some latent cultural identity on Dad's part or simply by a preference in taste? Or might it have been a largely economic decision, tea being less expensive than coffee?

That financial reality dictated, I'm sure, when our home would finally have the enjoyment of television. The excuse for the delay was always that we would wait until it was available in color. Meanwhile, until a TV was purchased, neighbors Elmer and Annie Holmberg often invited my parents into their home on Monday evenings to watch *I Love Lucy*,[7] while I attended meetings of Boy Scout Troop #45 at First Lutheran Church.

A decision, mutually made before their marriage but prompted largely by Dad's foresight, amazes me for its rationale. The decision was that Mom would quit her better-paying job while Dad, with his lesser-paying job, would be the sole financial provider. The reason, however, was not what might have been expected for the late 1930s: A woman's place was in the home. Instead, the reason, which seems surprising for its practicality but more for its insight into the human tendency of clinging to patterns of behavior once begun, was that should the day come when Mom would prefer or need to be at home on a full-time basis, it would be best never to have become accustomed to two incomes.

That decision having been made, their life together was begun on Dad's wage of thirty cents an hour. Twenty-nine years later upon his retirement, his hourly earnings had reached $1.95, the minimum wage in 1966 being $1.25. I remember the dried beef gravy on toast, sometimes garnished with peas, in the early years; how the times Dad's painting of the house outnumbered the times someone was hired for the job; and Mom putting off buying a new dress. Still, what I'll never fully comprehend is how they accomplished so much on so little.

And that included having and raising me, their only child. I suppose most only children wonder at some point about their relative solitude. Though I have wondered, I've never dwelled on it. The closest I ever came to pressing either of my parents on the subject was when I was a teenager. I commented to Mom how odd I thought it that, often, adults who were good parents didn't have more children. She gave no definitive response.

Many years later, in December 1997 and only three months prior to her ninetieth birthday, Mom said in an on-camera conversation for posterity taped by her grandson, "And *you*, Dan, were no accident!" I had long known that, but it was good to hear it spoken and with such emphasis.

The day came when I would leave my boyhood home. Mom and Dad would remain. That they felt they had everything in each other there is no question. Not long after my father's death, a quotation attributed to Winston Churchill turned up framed in Mom's apartment. It reads:

"My marriage was much the most fortunate and joyous event which happened to me in the whole of my life, for what can be more glorious than to be united in one's walk through life with a being incapable of an ignoble thought."

Churchill's words clearly reflected my mother's feelings about the man to whom she had been married for fifty-two years, the man who knew of her early disappointment in love and whose words, "I would like to try to make you happy," helped her move from an experience of tremendous loss to making room for, as she many years later would write, "Balm for a broken heart."

CHAPTER 3

A Time for Equanimity

For everything there is a season, and a time for every
matter under heaven: a time to weep, and a time to
laugh; a time to mourn, and a time to dance.
—Ecclesiastes 3:1, 4 (NRSV)

The ancient writer reminds us that a lifetime presents a rich assortment of experiences. Being born and dying have their times, as do waging war and making peace. Granted, he does ask, "What gain have the workers from their toil?" (Eccl. 3:9 NRSV) But as complete as the whole list is, equanimity is not included.

In January 1938, the orderlies at the Jamestown General Hospital were given a modest raise in hourly wage, bringing their weekly pay to $17.50. They were paid biweekly, each paycheck amounting to $35.00 minus deductions. Apparently, their raise was singular that year because other workers employed by the city were not so recognized.

However, the efforts of the hospital superintendent who had promoted a raise for the orderlies were, in the end, for naught. Once hearing of the orderlies' good fortune, certain city workers who had received no raise objected, their objection being forceful enough so that the raise was rescinded. In addition, the increase in pay already received was to be returned. In Mom's financial records, there's an old pay envelope advertising The National Chautauqua County Bank of Jamestown. "You Earned It—Now Save It," it encourages, with the added reminder: "No man ever became rich by spending all he earned." Obviously, and not surprisingly, inclusive language was to be decades into the future.

The total noted on the front of the envelope is $28.14. The back of the envelope breaks down the total:

Amount	$35.00
State Pension	$2.06
Overtime Deduction	$4.80
Balance	$28.14

What an ironic use of language—overtime *deduction*. It strikes me as a precursor to the more modern description *downward mobility*. In Dad's handwriting the date 10-21-38 appears on the envelope, as does this note in Mom's writing: "Overtime deduction went on for some time. It was taking back a raise given in January 1938."

As that year came to a close, Dad's weekly pay had decreased from $17.50 to $14.07. Although I never heard of it in their conversations, I did learn many years later from Mom that, as she said, "Now and then there was overtime pay for which we were grateful."

Mom and Dad's anxiety and frustration must have increased all the more with the expectation of my birth at year's end. It wasn't as though they'd been saving the raise with an inkling that it would someday be returned.

How an individual reacts to the ignoble actions of others usually sheds light on his or her character. The 10-21-38 pay envelope in my parents' financial records itself indicates what a blow the city's decision to rescind the raise *and* require its repayment was to their spirit, at least temporarily. Yet I suspect that Dad handled it with equanimity. Whenever the subject came up in later years, it was Mom who raised it. At the time, it was undoubtedly difficult for her to maintain calmness, as it was she who pored over the budget's figures each month, trying to make ends meet. But Dad would have more easily mixed the moment's sorrow, and perhaps tears, with an inner calm, believing that one simply had to look ahead a few months to the day when the paycheck would be at least even with its total prior to January 1. Being fair to the writer earlier quoted, the text does include: "a time to seek, and a time to lose" (Eccl. 3:6a NRSV).

He would have maintained such a view not only because he was a person of faith—not that Mom wasn't—but because by nature he looked on the bright side of things. He was, after all, just a year into marriage with the woman he loved, and their child was soon to be born.

As nasty as it was, the injustice of how city bureaucrats handled a pay raise's revocation was a momentary setback. While having everything was not without its trials, overall the future looked bright. That would have been Dad's perspective, a perspective that was fed by an event he and Mom experienced very likely at the time those pay deductions were occurring.

The weekend was approaching, and both food and funds were in meager supply. As Mom once told me the story, there was no assurance there would be food on the table come the approaching weekend. Too proud to approach either set of parents, they were facing what to them was a new and unsettling reality.

Then, a day or two before Sunday, Dad was approached by an acquaintance. Whether they simply met by chance on the street or the fellow was a visitor at the hospital, I don't know. But he was an area farmer, and he invited Dad to stop by the farm as he had some items he wanted to share. Probably borrowing his father's pickup truck as he sometimes did, Dad went to the farm. Upon returning to their apartment, Mom's prayers must have been fulfilled by what Dad had been given. Come Sunday, when they sat down at the table and were faced with what Mom had prepared—a stark contrast to what they had anticipated not many hours earlier—they wept.

That story, that real story prompts me to be even more struck by what today is a less than friendly attitude, not to mention an honest awareness, on the part of far too many legislators regarding the poor among us. Admittedly, there are those in our communities who will, as is said, work the system. Yet it has still to be shown that by far the majority of the poor, especially *the children*, are anything but genuinely poor and therefore, without assistance, often hungry.

In a humane society, does not the larger community, whether local, state, or national, have a responsibility toward those among us who are disadvantaged? Or are they, the disadvantaged, to rely solely on their own sense of equanimity? Contemporary Christian and novelist Marilynne Robinson says, "Patriotism is, first of all, an obligation to create humane circumstances within our country."[8] And as former President Jimmy Carter attests: "If you don't want your tax dollars to help the poor, then stop saying that you want a country based on Christian values. Because you don't!"[9]

Yes, the preceding two paragraphs are political in nature and therefore the stuff of debate, indeed, of controversy. And it is likewise true that an increase in financial assets alone, while possibly putting food on more tables, does not by itself assure happiness. I recall having read that, as this new century began and in the midst of a momentary economic upswing, Google searches for "happiness" in fact increased by a considerable percentage.

Dad's happiness, it was always clear, centered on relationship—that with his Creator and his family—relationship that he understood to be both essential and secure, however unpredictable otherwise the circumstances of daily life.

CHAPTER 4

———◆◦◆———

6 Charles Street

1600 Pennsylvania Avenue NW
10 Downing Street
6 Charles Street

6 *what?* And *where?* The first two addresses are perhaps recognizable to a majority of people on planet earth, and without further explanation. The same cannot be said of the third address.

I clearly recall that at the wedding of Charles, Prince of Wales, and Lady Diana Spencer on July 29, 1981, the preacher in his homily made a comment to the effect that, however humble a dwelling might be, it is the occupants' castle. In the usual sense of the word, 6 Charles Street was no castle. Yet in contrast to the one-level apartment at 211 Prospect Street where Mom and Dad had lived since marrying, it was a two-story house.

And how they loved that little house! When my parents first became interested in it, it was in such a state of disrepair that it would have been an embarrassment for most people even to consider buying it. Indeed, one of Dad's brothers said, "I wouldn't take that house as a gift." Dad's response was, "You won't have to; *we* are going to buy that house and live in it."

The most poignant encounter, however, was between Mom and her father-in-law. Grandpa Carlson visited her on a day and during hours when Dad was at work, all but pleading that his son and daughter-in-law rid themselves of any notion of purchasing the unkempt house. Grandpa and Grandma lived at 114 William Street; while not in the same neighborhood, it was but a brief twenty-minute walk between the two addresses. "Anyone who would live in that house," said Grandpa, "is either so poor they can't help themselves, or they don't care how they live." Might the relatively close proximity have influenced Grandpa's harsh judgment? "Well, Mr. Carlson," Mom replied, "that's exactly the situation we're in—so poor that we can't help ourselves." She added that the house in question was just within their reach financially, and therefore they would require no help in the reaching.

It was 1940. The house cost $1,500. Mom and Dad borrowed the money from an older couple in the church who, it was widely known, had money to lend. The only collateral was the word of the church custodian, who assured the lenders that he himself would make good on the debt should that become necessary.

The house's layout was ordinary. The front door led into the living room, to the right of which was a small room that held an old pump organ, Mom's sewing machine, and, besides a small desk and the telephone, not much else.

Opposite the front door, the living room led into the dining room on the left and into the kitchen on the right. A tiny bathroom was adjacent to the kitchen, as was an enclosed back porch housing a gas burner that was used every Monday morning for heating water to wash clothes. The presence of a washboard or two also hinted at one of the porch's primary functions.

The upstairs provided just enough space for two bedrooms and a small walk-in attic. The cellar, which was accessible from both the kitchen and an outside entrance, was distinguished by a dirt floor and what I remember to have been a stone cistern, long in disuse by the time we became occupants.

The living room was enhanced by a bay window set in the middle of the wall to the left of the front door. Each December, from my birthday on the nineteenth to New Year's Day, the Christmas tree filled that window setting. With its bright lights and glistening tinsel, it offered a sense of magic for those few days.

When purchased, the house, both inside and outside, was badly in need of work. The backyard appeared to have been used by the former occupants and perhaps by neighbors as a dumping ground for all sorts of things while the house had stood unoccupied. But by the time our family moved from there nine years later the place had been transformed. At the front of the house both sides had been graced by a white picket fence built by Grandpa Haskell, built no doubt in part to assure that his young grandson would not wander alone into the front yard, or worse, the street. The backyard was now, to a young boy's eyes, a large fenced-in grassy area, bordered on one side by a beautiful flower garden that occasionally provided snips of grass onion that in turn spiced a milk-based gravy. A small rock garden was nestled into a corner of the yard's shady far end.

The usual face-lifting had been done to the inside as well, including the addition of a French door in the living room at the bottom of the stairway leading upstairs. To the right of that doorway stood the Moore gas heater, the only source of heat in the house, above which was a register that provided a modicum of heat for one of the two upstairs bedrooms. But that register also provided a conduit for my hearing the conversation of adult voices during late evening hours after I had been sent to bed, especially on occasions when Mom and Dad were entertaining.

It was a small and, in time, charming house that at first prompted derision from certain of my parents' peers as well as the anguished plea of the older generation, but then was transformed into a castle just big enough for three. The elegance of the French door, juxtaposed with the relative simplicity, if not primitiveness, of the gas space heater and the ceiling register above it, together spoke of a time and of a place that today seem so distant and yet so memorable.

Nearly four decades later, on the day Charles and Diana exchanged vows in London's St. Paul's Cathedral, Mom and Dad, by then having long lived in a very different setting, went downtown for lunch in celebration of the royal nuptials. As they enjoyed the moment, perhaps having heard the homily from St. Paul's, I wonder to what extent their minds wandered back to the years of life in their first modest castle. Certainly that had been a time in their life together when having almost nothing did not exclude the possibility of having nearly everything.

CHAPTER 5

The Power of Suggestion and Belief

O, this is the great joy of which the angel speaks. This is the comfort and exceeding goodness of God that, if a man believes this, he can boast of the treasure that Mary is his rightful mother, Christ his brother, and God his father. For these things actually occurred and are true, but we must believe. This is the principal thing and the principal treasure in every Gospel, before any doctrine of good works can be taken out of it. Christ must above all things become our own and we become his, before we can do good works.[10]—Martin Luther

---

Dad was not without a religious background, his Swedish immigrant parents having assured his baptism into the Christian faith on April 25, 1897. He had also gone through the preparation for and finally the Lutheran Rite of Confirmation. Just how much he frequented the magnificent church building and the worship that took place there by the time he was into adulthood, I am uncertain.

I do know that in his early adult years, Dad smoked cigars, as did several of the Carlson males. One Saturday evening, when Dad was on his way to a downtown movie theater, he met an acquaintance who suggested that instead of the theater Dad accompany him to the Salvation Army where an evangelist from Sweden was holding forth. (Historically, it has not been uncommon for non-Lutherans to feel that Lutherans are in need of a spiritual awakening.) Probably to satisfy the neighbor acquaintance, Dad changed direction, smoking as he went. Then, not wanting to waste what was left of a perfectly good cigar, he snuffed it out and put it into his coat pocket upon entering the place of meeting.

Whatever happened at that meeting caused Dad, upon exiting, to throw away what was left of the snuffed-out cigar. He never smoked again, though he did remain a Lutheran, an increasingly active one in parish life as the years progressed. In fact, it was shortly after the Salvation Army experience—one that his sister, Adeline, says "touched his heart"—when the pastor of the congregation, Dr. Samuel Miller,[11] having learned of it, contacted Dad and asked that he be a teacher in the Sunday church school. And in January 1937 he was elected to the congregation's Board of Deacons.

All of this, of course, influenced the person I one day would become. But in terms of a piece of the healthy environment in which I was raised, I've always credited the Salvation Army and the Swedish evangelist with my having grown up in a smoke-free home.

There is no question but that Dad both understood and experienced the faith in personal terms. I can see him kneeling at his bedside in prayer. Whether a daily practice or not, the mind's image of that posture conveys forcefully a belief in a Creator who is yet mindful of his creation, of his creatures.

Luther speaks to the personal when again he reflects on the angel's words in Luke 2:10–11 (NRSV), the angel announcing, "I am bringing you good news of great joy for all the people." Says Luther: "The little word 'you' should make us joyful. For unto whom does He speak? Unto wood or stones? Nay, verily, He speaks unto men; and not unto one or two, but unto all the people. How then shall we understand these words? Shall we yet doubt the grace of God and say: 'St. Peter and St. Paul may well rejoice that their Saviour is come, but I may not, I am a wretched sinner; the dear and precious treasure is not for me!'? My friend, if thou wilt say: He is not mine, then shall I say: Whose is He then? Has He come to save geese and ducks and cows? Thou must look here who He is. If He had come to save another creature, yea, of a truth, He had assumed the likeness of that creature. But now He hath been made the Son of Man."[12]

Within a few years of what must be considered my father's awakening, or conversion, experience, he would write in his diary, dated December 31, 1967, during a Christmastide visit to West Warwick, Rhode Island, where I was serving my first parish, Emanuel Lutheran Church: "We attended church this morning. I sure enjoy to hear our Dan preach and sing. It really comes from the heart. You are wonderful, Faith. We love all three of you so much." The third of "all three" was our son, Curtis, our first child born seven months earlier. Carolyn was to be born three years later.

Later in these pages is a brief review of Dad's own experience of being a long-term patient in a hospital when compared to most hospital stays today. His youngest sibling having been three years of age at the time, her knowledge today of the episode is the result of having been told by others. But besides what is already noted above, what she reports in a later chapter of the effect on her eldest brother of the evening at the Salvation Army indicates that experience to have come at a later point both in his and in her life than did the hospitalization.

From the angel's "you," to Luther's emphasis of same, to my father's belief in the One of whom the angel spoke, Dad lived the faith both in his love for his family and in the vocation he ultimately was led to choose.

CHAPTER 6

———◦•◦———

An Iron of a Different Kind and Service in a Different Theater

We had lived in the house on Charles Street three or four years, and the replacement of the eave troughs and downspouts could no longer be put off. Dad, having learned the sheet metal business from his father, could do much of the work himself. Memory tells me that he tackled the job during a week of summer vacation. I don't recall whether he had help with all the cutting and forming of the required pieces. What I do remember is Dad assembling the pieces there on the front lawn. Of particular fascination to me was his use of the soldering iron, that Iron Age–like instrument for attaching metal to metal. The small but noisy blaze in the fire pot, the long-handled iron being fired in the pot, the jar of acid, and the stick of hard solder: I can see and hear and almost smell it all these seventy years later.

Dad loved his home, but he was not especially domestic or even generally very handy around the house. He was certainly helpful, never hesitating to dry dishes or to assist in the kitchen. His unique contribution in the latter instance was the coffee, which he made with the addition of an egg—or was it with one or the other part of an egg?—to enhance the brew's clarity. Probably due to economic necessity, Dad agreed with Mom that such a specialty would occur only when entertaining.

I doubt, however, whether Dad ever ironed a shirt after May 30, 1937, and probably never before either. Yet, while words such as *artisan, craftsman,* or even *tradesman* were not in my childhood vocabulary, I knew when watching him make the hard solder molten by the use of the fired iron, then skillfully fasten the seam of two pieces of metal, that I was watching something, and someone, special.

There are fired irons of the kind just described, and there are fired irons of the kind used in warfare. Dad, in his midforties, was not engaged in either the European or Pacific theaters of World War II. But engaged he was.

I have a young boy's vivid memories of that war's several years. On a Sunday afternoon when visiting Grandma Haskell, Grandpa Haskell called from the fire station where he was working the day shift, saying that a troop train was passing by. It was heading east to New York City. Ladder Company #4 was located across the street from tracks of the Erie Railroad. And I remember once or twice seeing Dad's brother, Uncle Oscar, in uniform as he was in town on leave. Another uncle, Robert Main, the then husband of Aunt Adeline, was an artist and drew maps for General Douglas McArthur.

Also, on June 10, 1945, a tornado went through part of town. One day shortly afterward, when walking with Mom from home to downtown, we came upon several military police where Barrett Avenue, Glasgow Avenue, Steele and Market Streets converged. Military police were guarding other men who were gathering storm-related debris. Later we learned that those being guarded were German prisoners of war. And most poignantly for our family was being aware of Mom's brother-in-law, my Uncle Art, deeply mourning the loss of his youngest brother, Harold Oberg, who was one of the casualties when the Dorchester, a troop ship, was sunk by German torpedoes on February 3, 1943. That incident quickly became iconic because of the four chaplains on board who gave up their life jackets so that others might possibly live. In the end, many who had life jackets did not survive due to the frigidness of the water.

Then, too, I recall the day groups of neighbors kept walking past our house and, when asked where they were going, they answered, "Downtown for the celebration!" The war had ended; it was 1945, and I suspect that whatever the weather might have been that day, those headed for downtown would have gone anyway. And whatever the exact date of that largely civilian gathering, surely it was summertime in their hearts.

Where was my dad in all of this? He was engaged in the at-home theater of the war. In a later chapter it is noted that on several occasions, in the middle of the night, he would go to the hospital, Civil Defense armband in place, for an air raid drill. Why would a city in western New York State have air raid drills? Because one of its factories turned out ball bearings and it was thought to be a potential bombing target. And how was the population of the city and the surrounding communities, numbering some fifty thousand souls, alerted that an air raid drill was beginning? Factory whistles would begin to sound—a very sudden and scary way to be awakened in the darkness, especially, as in my case, at an early age. I would say to my parents at bedtime, "If there's an air raid drill, please come into my room!"

There was one more way Dad participated in the war effort. I can see and almost hear him stepping on and flattening empty tin cans that had held soup, fruit, or a vegetable. Citizens were asked to supply those flattened receptacles, which then were recycled for use in the war effort.

No doubt, too, during those years Dad practiced what his diary records him doing some two decades later. On April 26, 1967, as the Vietnam conflict continued, he recorded: "Thank God for all the blessings we have in our country. We need to pray for the whole world and our boys in the war and their boys also." By "their boys" I'm certain Dad meant the enemy. He would have been familiar with Jesus' words in Matthew's gospel:

"You have heard that it was said, 'You shall love your neighbor and hate your enemy.' But I say to you, Love your enemies and pray for those who persecute you, so that you may be children of your Father in heaven; for he makes his sun rise on the evil and on the good, and sends rain on the righteous and on the unrighteous." (Matt. 5:43–45 NRSV)

Definitely, Dad would have remembered in prayer both parties in the conflict. That was my dad.

CHAPTER 7

He Who Carried Me and Remained Present

It was early summer 1945. Mom and I were at Grandma and Grandpa Carlson's, visiting with an aunt and cousin who had arrived from California. Cousin Beverly and I were outside playing when Mom called me inside. Word had just been received, probably from Dad, who would have telephoned from the hospital, that I had been diagnosed with a kidney infection—actually, with puss in the kidneys—yes, a nasty sounding infection, and it was that and more.

The remainder of the summer was spent either in bed or on the couch in the living room, receiving regular doses of sulfa, the only drug at the time known to be effective in that situation. Come early September I was permitted to begin first grade, although a week or two after classes had begun.

Given when the illness struck me, it was probably the most serious illness I've ever had. I can still hear the pediatrician, Dr. Kelley, say to my mother once I appeared to have overcome the infection, "Danny has been a very sick boy." At the age of six I had no idea how serious my condition had been.

Besides especially Mom's care at home during those summer weeks, I remember receiving, as a special treat from my Aunt Anne on the other side of the state, a little jar of homemade jam. It was so good when spread on toast that, even when it was gone and the jar was empty, I would sniff the jar! Mostly, however, these words are about neither the summer of '45 nor gifted jam, but about the instances when I was a patient at the hospital, and Dad was on the orderly staff.

I was the recipient of Dad's attention while in the hospital a total of five times. Beginning at age three when I had surgery on a congenital hernia and through two episodes while in high school involving implacable ingrown nails on my great toes, Dad was there. In the 1950s, even the minor surgical attention given those toes included an overnight stay at the hospital.

A fourth instance was the common tonsillectomy, an episode that included several penicillin injections in the buttocks, moments that I dreaded because of what I felt as severe pain. Just at the sight of the approaching nurse and her harpoon, commonly known as a syringe, I could be heard probably on the next floor. While I was too frightened to be embarrassed by the commotion I was causing, no doubt my dad was relieved when finally I was discharged. So traumatic was the memory of those injections that, some ten years later, during an appointment with an otolaryngologist, the good physician approached me with a syringe, one that probably held penicillin. My reaction must have been sufficiently impressive, because he dismissed me without following through.

I'm fairly certain that, both for the hernia and tonsillectomy surgeries, Dad was with me while the anesthesia was administered, assuring my young spirit as much emotional calm as possible.

It was a fifth incident, however, that remains the most memorable in terms of my relationship with my dad. It was a hot summer day, and the tar near the curb in front of the house on Charles Street was soft, not unlike warm Play-doh. At some point during the afternoon, I'd had my hands in that tar, something that a four- or five-year-old might be tempted to do. No doubt Mom had cleaned my hands as thoroughly as she could. Still, at some point during the nighttime hours, I awakened from significant pain. One of my fingers had become infected.

Our house being located but a fifteen-to-twenty minute walk from the hospital, Dad carried me from home to there in the early morning hours. I can recall being in a children's ward bed, a physician present, and Dad standing by. This time it was not a syringe that I saw gleaming as the directed light shown on my finger, but rather what appeared to be an instrument similar to a scalpel. The physician lanced the finger and then dressed it.

I'm sure that the combination of the pain and having Dad present gave me an acceptance of what had to be done, an acceptance I would otherwise have lacked. That children were sleeping in nearby beds also no doubt caused me to somehow keep my cries to a loud whimper at the knife's anticipated penetration. As I remember the incident now, it very likely occurred at an earlier date than the tonsillectomy, and thus I would not yet have been familiar with its related injections.

Today, having long since been a parent and also a grandparent, I can imagine how Dad must have been in pain with me. We hurt for, and sometimes with, our children. A mentor of mine once said, "We're never happier than our least happy child." Today, while the scar on the tar-infected finger is long gone, the blessed memory of my father's loving arms that carried me from home to the hospital, and of his faithful presence by the bedside, remains.

CHAPTER 8

Trauma on the New York Central and on the Streets of Albany

Long trips were uncommon in our family. Without a car, short trips were also infrequent. For the latter, we depended on the thoughtfulness of friends and extended family. Mother's sister, Gladys Oberg, and her husband, Arthur, often included us in Sunday afternoon rides up to the lake or down to Kinzua, a major dam and reservoir project engineered at midcentury that tamed the Allegheny River in northwestern Pennsylvania. Mom, Dad, and I were always grateful whenever the going-out-for-a-ride plans of others included us.

However, the summer of 1946 saw us on an unusual trip, one which for us was a major undertaking. Earlier in the year a younger brother of Dad's, Augard, and his wife, Anne, invited us to eastern New York for a brief visit. That such a trip was affordable remains something of a mystery. Mom's meticulous financial records give no clue, but perhaps Uncle Augie and Aunt Anne sent money for the train tickets.

To get to the New York Central terminal in Westfield, New York, we first had to ride the Jamestown-Westfield trolley, the J-W. The J-W had a track that ran adjacent to Chautauqua Lake's northeastern shoreline; that was also a means to get to church picnics in my early childhood. But now it was to take us to Westfield, where we would board the *big* train.

Once on the train, I was seated across from Mom and Dad, on the aisle but a row or two behind them. Not long into the trip I saw the conductor coming down the aisle, inspecting and punching tickets and then turning officially to the next passenger. I soon realized that, compared to his encounters with other passengers, the conductor's conversation with my parents was taking unusually long. Even more telling was the expressions of palpable concern that clouded their faces as they looked up at the authoritative man impressively dressed in black. It seemed that the reservations agent in Jamestown had made an error in the ticketing and, the conductor said, "I could have the three of you put off the train right now." That would have made it a very short trip indeed, since the train had not yet gone as far as Buffalo.

Why the conductor didn't have us put off the train at the next stop, I still don't know. Perhaps he sensed our unseasoned travelers' innocence and embarrassment, choosing not to compound the error of a distracted ticket agent. Or perhaps, like Dad, he was simply a compassionate man.

The first thing Uncle Augie did upon our arrival in Albany was to have the tickets for our return trip to Jamestown checked for their validity. One trauma was behind us.

Uncle Augie and Aunt Anne's home was in suburban Slingerlands, where we were treated wonderfully. Their hospitality included day trips both to Bennington, Vermont, where we visited the three hundred-plus-foot stone obelisk erected in commemoration of the Battle of Bennington during the American Revolution—that, as well as to Lake George, where we enjoyed a ride in a glass-bottom boat. However, sheer suspense awaited us on the day when Uncle Augie went to his New York Telephone Company office in Albany. He'd need to be picked up at the end of the day, and Aunt Anne asked Dad to drive us all into the city so we could get a taste of downtown and see where his brother worked.

Why it fell to Dad to drive remains unclear. It wasn't that my aunt didn't drive. I'm assured by my cousin, Betty, that her mother was a seasoned driver and that, while she had a feminist side, she was also thoughtful. Did she think her brother-in-law would get a kick out of driving in a big city or, perhaps, that he'd be offended if not asked to drive?

I remember Dad protesting the idea that he should drive into downtown Albany at any time of day, let alone during the rush hour. It wasn't that he didn't drive. He still maintained his license, if for no other reason than occasionally to borrow the truck from the family sheet metal business. The problem was that he hadn't yet driven a vehicle with the standard transmission shift on the steering wheel column.

But we were guests, and Aunt Anne was reassuring. "I'll help," she kept insisting, and in the end Dad acquiesced. How he must have been steeling himself for what lay ahead!

The ride from outlying Slingerlands was uneventful. Upon reaching the downtown area, however, Dad became tense, and what were probably only a few blocks to my uncle's office building must have seemed like a cross-country drive to him.

Mom and I were in the back seat. Aunt Anne was in the front passenger seat from where she would lean toward Dad, ordering him to depress the clutch while she grabbed the gearshift. In such fashion, we went lurching from light to light and from block to block, once coming close to striking a curb.

The two back seat passengers knew that all was not well, but we were helpless. Aunt Anne's sheer determination to get to her husband's office with Dad at the wheel apparently gave her courage. And my poor dad probably hadn't been so traumatized since the day, many years earlier, when he'd fallen backward off a horse-drawn grocery delivery wagon, striking the back of his head on the hard pavement and bounding back onto the wagon without the driver ever knowing he'd momentarily lost his assistant. In those desperate moments, in the relative congestion of downtown Albany on an otherwise lovely summer afternoon, I suspect that Dad would gladly have exchanged what he was doing for a second fall from the grocery wagon. The experience may also have sealed the reality of his having white hair by the time he was age fifty.

Finally, and without police intervention or worse, our by now unnerved quartet arrived at Uncle Augie's office building. The ordeal predated the use of the word *trauma* in everyday speech, but that absence in no way diminished what we had just been through. Dad's "Boy, I'm glad that's over!" was echoed by Aunt Anne's "Is Chandler ever glad to see you!" once Uncle Augie was in the car and behind the wheel. We *all* were glad!

CHAPTER 9

---•◦•---

"Honestly!"
An Incongruity Episode

I was lying above the bedroom floor register, feeling the gentle and comforting drift of heat rising from the space heater below, listening and feeling guilty for not actually being in my bed but not guilty enough to leave my advantageous post. The voices below were those of Mom and Dad and two of their friends, Wilton and Alice Strand. The five of us had not long before returned from a concert by the Jamestown Civic Orchestra.

Both of the Strands, whom we knew through the church, were employed by a local bank, Alice herself being a trust officer, a role, I understood at the time, few women by then had achieved. There was laughter, Alice saying, "Wasn't it funny how she said, 'Honestly?'" The laughter was good to hear, as earlier in the evening the Strands had driven us to the concert in their new car. When Mom inquired as to the make of the car and having been told it was a Chevrolet, she said, "Oh, you bought a cheap one." Wilton responded quickly and with emphasis, saying, *"Cheap?* This car *cost* two thousand dollars!"

But now there was laughter. *She*, I remembered, was a concert-goer who had been seated directly in front of us and with whom Dad had come in physical contact while getting into our row of seats. Perhaps she was wearing a hat—women wore hats in the 1940s—and Dad had disturbed that. But whatever he had done to affront her, her reaction had been an audible "Honestly!" And now, while enjoying coffee and whatever else Mom had prepared, they laughed, my parents and their guests.

I don't think they were laughing at the hapless, and perhaps momentarily hatless, woman so much as they were laughing at the situation. Dad, of all people, was not one to go out of his way to elicit an "Honestly!" from anyone, least of all at a formal community gathering. Just the opposite was the case. His demeanor was that of a person trying his best not to offend. So it was the incongruity of the moment that was at first startling, then amusing, and finally, there in the living room beneath the upstairs bedroom floor register, laughable.

Sixty years or so later an equally humorous moment occurred at St. Peter's Lutheran Church, Newport, Rhode Island, where I was briefly serving as transitional pastor. It was early 2007, and the Strands' only child, Donald, and his wife, Lynn, visited us on a Sunday, first meeting us at the church for the morning service. Donald, three years my junior, had asked that I be his best man when he and Lynn married forty years earlier.

In the mid-1960s, Donald had served in the Navy, briefly being stationed in Newport. While there he would attend St. Peter's Church. Now, on this Sunday in 2007 and when introducing the couple to the congregation, I reviewed that history. A lay leader then asked Donald how long it had been since he'd visited the church. "About forty years," he answered. Being a congregation that historically had both depended on and enjoyed Navy personnel among its membership, the response to Donald was, "Might you return a bit sooner next time?" In that setting, the exchange resulted in a hearty chuckle from the congregation.

In contrast to the episode involving the elder Strands and Mom and Dad, the more recent Newport incident represented congruity, the linkage between the generations, partly nourished by an essential element of human relationship, indeed even of survival, namely that of humor.

CHAPTER 10

Through a Class Dimly

It was a Sunday morning in the early 1950s, and Dad, my two cousins, Tom and Elaine, and I had walked to the car following worship, several minutes ahead of Mom and my Aunt Gladys. Only my aunt had the keys to the car, so we were left to wait there in the parking lot of the globally-known Crescent Tool Company, with the railroad tracks and the length of a city block separating us from the towering church structure, the size of which seemed to increase when viewed from a distance. In retrospect, I see the scene as medieval in its symbolism: the hugeness of the Romanesque church building towering over its neighborhood of modest houses as well as over a variety of factory buildings further down the hill.

Dad had wandered away from my cousins and me. When we looked over at him, he was slightly stooped, his hands shielding his eyes as he peered into a factory window some twenty yards away. What could he be looking for, my cousins and I wondered. What did he expect the Sabbath silence on the other side of the grimy window to reveal?

But it wasn't what he was looking *for*. It was what he was looking *at* that caught his attention. When he came back to the car, he said,

"Oh, boy! They have *some* machinery in there!" That was so like him, to be impressed, even delighted, by the ordinary and also by the work of others. We would be downtown, and he would notice the detailed masonry work high up on some of the older buildings. "Oh, boy! Look at that work up there!" he'd say in amazement.

Sometimes we have to shade the light from our eyes, and sometimes we don't. In either case, just to be looking at the tools others work with, such as through a factory window in the relative stillness of a Sunday morning, or at the result of another's work, such as a stone mason's artistry, is to be both aware and appreciative of the world beyond oneself. Dad was aware of that world, and he never hesitated to voice both his wonder and appreciation.

That from which Dad shielded his eyes, and also his awareness and appreciation of the world beyond himself, serves as apt though limited metaphor for his daily work at the hospital. In that setting he neither shielded his eyes nor saw dimly but rather, with clarity of both sight and purpose, he responded to the needs of patients to whom he was assigned.

The wonder with which he was struck by the sight of unfamiliar machinery or the result of a stone mason's work—that same wonder in the hospital was generated by fellow human beings with whom he would interact. And interact not as if at the post office or on the commuter bus, but in situations when sometimes life itself hung in the balance. In that place and in those moments, often it was not Dad but the patient who was seeing as through a glass dimly, who might shield the eyes from a procedure he or she preferred not watching.

Life consists of encounters with both the animate and inanimate, each making life all that it is. Dad's greatest joy came from, and his lasting influence was imparted on, the animate, on fellow travelers whose journey momentarily required, whether a quiet word or a soothing touch, healing attention.

CHAPTER 11

---•◆•---

In His Grip

An example of my dad's restraint in situations that in many other parents might easily cause anger, or certainly a harsh reprimand, happened when I was about seven years old. The setting was our Charles Street residence. Mom was out on a brief errand, Dad was at work, and I was home alone.

What prompted my interest in matches and flame, I'm uncertain; but in Mom's absence I emptied a small metal can of its marbles, replaced them with paper, and engaged the paper with a flaming match. It probably did not burn for more than sixty seconds before it was more smoke than flame. And then the top of the can was put back in its proper place.

Mom returned home. She wasn't in the house more than a minute or two before she went from room to room, sniffing the air, very much like a dog just beginning its first outside walk of the day. I soon owned up to my potentially disastrous activity. My immediate punishment? To look at a humanlike illustration of Satan as depicted in a book of Bible stories—and told to think about the force that had prompted my playing with fire.

And my Dad's reaction once he was home from work? His was

more response than reaction. There was a mild scolding, of course; he agreeing with Mom as to the seriousness of what I had done. Yet I've always attributed his restraint in that instance to his thankfulness that the house itself was still standing.

A senior acquaintance once told me of his father, "He never laid a hand on me." It was clear from the tenor of his voice and from the expression on his face that he felt his father's restraint had been an attribute. Cousin Elaine's son, Karl Mattson, now well into adulthood, has said of my father, "I cannot imagine him being angry."

As for physical contact, Dad practiced the same restraint toward me as already noted. There was one instance, however, when I did hear and feel his anger expressed toward me. In fact, it was an instance when he put both his hands on me. It happened at the end of a family gathering when, due to early adolescent impertinence, I said something rude to my mother. Immediately, while still in the presence of others, Dad took hold of both my forearms with his hands and in as stern a voice as I'd ever heard from him—or would ever hear again—made it clear that speaking to my mother in such a way was unacceptable. What he said did not impress me nearly as much as the force of his grip on my forearms. It was a singular incident.

Although he was slight of build, Dad's arms were well developed. First there had been the lifting of the ladders and sheet metal when working with his father and brothers. Then, and especially in the early years of his work at the hospital, before manually operated hydraulic lifts came into use, literal manual lifting of patients was the norm. Whether moving a patient closer to the bed's headboard; or transferring a patient from bed to a chair or from gurney to an operating table and later back to bed or to the gurney; or supporting a patient requiring steadiness of feet following a prolonged stay in the prone position; muscle strength of the attending person was regularly tested. And how comforting for the patient to sense that the attendant was physically matched to the task.

Thus, by the 1950s, when he chose to make a point by the physical strength available to him, as he did that once, Dad's force was appreciable. It was not, however, abusive use of strength. Instead, it was a sudden, reactive show of resolve that his spouse was not to be abused by either the attitude or the words of their son.

Regarding abuse in contrast to resolve as I experienced it, I recall in my own ministry once advising a distraught woman early into marriage that vows taken in a Christian setting need not entrap a person in an abusive relationship.

How different some news reports today would read and sound if those husbands and fathers who physically abuse spouses and children were instead convinced of the futility guaranteed, not to mention the immorality shown, by such actions. Granted, often the behavior making headlines and creating shelters for those abused stems as much from deep emotional imbalance as from personal issues seemingly requiring only a court-ordered anger management course, albeit a thin line seeming to separate the two.

Still, in communities both local and of global proportion beset by at best impaired judgment and at worst almost unimaginable violence, how basic, how very needed are family settings that model healthy human interaction, settings where tension is fostered by disagreement and misunderstanding yet in which abuse is absent.

As I remember that solitary incident between my father and me, now some six decades later, I am grateful as well as impressed: impressed that even today my surprise at his grip reminds me that his emotions had such capacity and grateful for his solidarity with my mother.

CHAPTER 12

———◆·◆·◆———

Celebrities on the Water

Beginning in 1828 and continuing into the mid-twentieth century, the waters of Chautauqua Lake were home to upward of a dozen passenger boats—steamers, as they were known to many—only one of which remained by the early 1950s. Gone were the days when the two-decker boats were used for transportation up and down the seventeen mile-long glacial melt. At the height of their service the boats would carry to hotel docks, as well as to picnic and entertainment sites, up to a quarter million passengers in a single season.[13] But now the lone survivor, aptly named City of Jamestown and a smaller version of other two-deckers that once had shared adjacent berths, was called upon for pleasure only.

Which was why, one summer day, our family decided to ride the boat to Bemus Point. Mom prepared a picnic lunch, and we took the bus to the boat landing, all set for an enjoyable several hours.

When we arrived for boarding, however, we were told that the boat was chartered for the day and so wouldn't be stopping at Bemus Point. The news caught us by surprise, because, uncharacteristically, Mom hadn't called ahead to check on the day's schedule. I don't remember exactly what happened next, but somehow the man in the ticket booth got word from the captain that we could board the boat. And the boat would even stop at Bemus Point, we were assured.

Being both confused and surprised, Mom, Dad, and I somewhat uncomfortably settled into some seats on the boat. Departure time arrived, deckhands freed the boat from the pier, and the boat's whistle—an inadequate word when I recall its majestic sound—blew several times, commanding attention for several blocks in every direction. We were underway.

It felt strange, knowing we were among a charter group of passengers. We recognized no one. *Did anyone wonder what we were doing there*, I remember thinking. Or was the group diverse enough itself so that others besides us went unrecognized? It didn't matter, for soon we were moving up the Chadakoin River outlet, and the closeness of the river's banks on either side heightened the expectancy of the much wider expanse of water that awaited us moments away.

Then we were there on the lake itself. It was a beautiful day to be on the water. The human voice sounded so different when in that atmosphere, muted by the droning of the ship's engines two decks below.

After passing through the lake's widest expanse, we could see Bemus Point in the distance. There was, and to this day remains, a ferry there—a cable-guided ferry the origins of which date back to 1811—crossing back and forth between Bemus Point on one side and Stow on the other. Its operator would have to adjust its schedule to permit passage for the Old Lady of the Lake, as the boat was nicknamed. Once through the narrows we would enter Bemus Bay, the captain steering the boat to the pier just beyond the classic Hotel Lenhart.

On this day, instead of sticking to the channel that would point the boat further up the lake to the charter group's destination, a decided turn to the starboard side caught passengers' attention. Our moment was at hand.

It's hard to describe the sensation of being given preferential treatment and simultaneously surprising a boatload of people. Not only was the boat making a special stop so we could disembark, but later in the day the captain would pilot the boat back into Bemus Bay, providing us the return trip. It would have been interesting to listen to the on-board buzz as the three of us left ship, and with picnic basket in tow, walked up the pier. But we heard none of it.

I'll always remember that day. And I've often wondered why the captain made the decision he did, appearing to make an exception for us. Was this another instance of Dad not recognizing someone who recognized him? Had the captain perhaps been a patient at the hospital, or had a member of his family been hospitalized and Dad was remembered for the care he had given? It might have been the simplest thing that he had done, but when you'll ill and in an unfamiliar environment, it's often the simplest thing that makes an otherwise anxiety-filled day less fearsome.

Whatever the captain's motivation, the result was the same. On a summer day in the early 1950s, a day just right for a ride on the lake, the same kind of celebrity treatment that Dad gave countless patients at the Jamestown General Hospital was returned to him and his family. And how fitting, too, that the boat itself should have had the name City of Jamestown, considering the choppy treatment—as in the lake's sometimes sudden and unsettling turbulence—the city itself had given several of its employees some fifteen years earlier.

Yes, it had been a *very* special day!

CHAPTER 13

---·◆·---

In College and So Much More

That his son was in college was a great source of satisfaction for my father. I left western New York for Nebraska in the fall of 1957, my leaving being the result, at least in part, of having stood in line once a week at the Charles Street School in the 1940s to purchase savings stamps, as they were called, which later could be cashed in for US Savings Bonds. For as little as Dad earned, the bulk of my eight years of college and theological education was financed by my parents.

It would have been unusual, then, had Dad, himself having completed only the sixth grade, not been proud that his son was in college. Mom told me when I was home the first Christmas that the pride came out in Dad's enunciation of "in college." They would be talking with friends, I would be mentioned, and Dad would say, "Yes, Dan's in col*lege*," with a uniquely distinct emphasis on the second syllable.

Such pride is largely a thing of the past, I think. Today, at least for many parents, pride at a child's being in college is being overshadowed if not eclipsed entirely by anxiety over how to pay for it—how to pay for it both during and after the college years themselves. It wasn't that my parents knew no anxiety over the costs of my schooling, possibly having concerns of which I have no knowledge. Still, the dominant reality for my dad, who by 1957 was sixty years old, was that a child of his was actually in col*lege.*

That reality of course led to much more, both in his life and in mine. Dad and Mom together attended my graduation from college and, four years later, from seminary. And remembering how proud and thankful my wife and I were when first our son, then our daughter, graduated from college, I can only imagine especially Dad's feelings when attending my ordination on June 9, 1965, at Trinity Lutheran Church, Stapleton, Staten Island, New York.

Some forty years later when leading a workshop in my home congregation while representing the Lutheran Planned Giving Consortium in New England, Uncle Phil, by then Dad's only surviving brother, was present. Following the program he said, "I've been thinking how proud your dad would be had he been here." Dad had died a little over a decade earlier.

Indeed, how proud. Dad, who himself was a young adult during The Great War, had raised a son whose earliest years were during World War II and who, in large part because of Dad's work at the hospital and Mom's consistent tracking of their finances, was now, while still a pastor, advising and assisting believers in matters addressing end-of-life financial stewardship. How could Dad, the eldest of eight children who had remained at home until age forty, possibly have anticipated not only the path his son's life would take but also the influence he himself ultimately would have in his son's vocational journey?

To be sure, both of my parents, each in their own way, were responsible for the encouragement I received after announcing by the time I was nine years of age that I wanted someday to be a pastor. But there is no doubt that my dad's own decades-long vocation, one of ministering to the ill, influenced me in ways of which still today I remain less than fully aware. My thirty-four years as a parish pastor, followed by the seven years as a financial gift planner, and in retirement working nearly two years part time for Lutheran Social Services of New England—in all of it my father's influence was present.

Yes, I had been in col*lege*. And how grateful I am today.

CHAPTER 14

His Awareness Enhanced

As extensive as was his world in the setting of the hospital—
especially given the number and variety of people with whom he
came in contact year-to-year over the span of thirty-six years—Dad
was aware of a world beyond the one in which white-clad people
served others.

Jamestown, being located at the lower end of the lake, the name
by which world-renowned Chautauqua Institution is also known,
has had access to wonderful opportunities for the enhancement of
one's interests, be they specifically spiritual, intellectual, musical
or any one of the three mutually related to the other two. During
its yearly summer season, Chautauqua offers a wide and inspiring
array of speakers, individual musicians, and musical groups for both
educational and entertainment purposes. The large amphitheater
itself, the Hall of Philosophy, Norton Memorial Hall, each is a setting
in which equally informative and stimulating programs are provided.

For example, in the summer of 1961, Dr. Karl Menninger of the
Menninger Clinic, Topeka, Kansas, spoke to a morning gathering
in the amphitheater, a gathering of which I was privileged to be a
part. His theme seemed almost impromptu, in that he leafed through

a morning newspaper, very possibly the *New York Times*, selecting articles as he came upon them, and then making comments on same. Not now recalling one article's specifics, it reported on an action of an individual that positively affected the life of another individual. Dr. Menninger noted how frequently one hears such an action being described as having been done by a "do-gooder" and often said as something less than a compliment. His response that morning was to ask, "Well, what would people prefer—do-*badders*?"

Although Dad was not present to hear Dr. Menninger, as time and opportunity permitted, both he and Mom took advantage of such opportunities, always having benefited from the thoughtfulness of others in providing the transportation. At some point during his four terms in office as governor of New York State, Nelson Rockefeller spoke to a full amphitheater. I can still hear him say that while people sometimes wonder why anyone would choose to go into politics, why wouldn't you go into politics, he asked, if you thought you could make a difference. Dad was present for that address.

Chautauqua has a long history of a chaplain of the week being part of the daily program. Most often the chaplain has been well known nationally, sometimes globally. On a Sunday not long after the end of World War II, specifically July 30, 1950, and into the first week of August, that person was Martin Niemoeller, the German Lutheran pastor to whom is attributed the following: "First they came for the Socialists, and I did not speak out—because I was not a Socialist. Then they came for the Trade Unionists, and I did not speak out—because I was not a Trade Unionist. Then they came for the Jews, and I did not speak out—because I was not a Jew. Then they came for me—and there was no one left to speak for me."[14] As an anti-Nazi activist and a founder of the Confessing Church, Niemoeller had experienced life not in one but in two concentration camps, the second having been Dachau, where he remained until the end of the war.[15] Dad was present to hear Dr. Niemoeller.

Accompanying Dr. Niemoeller to Chautauqua was his wife, who also made several presentations during the week.

Similarly, our congregation provided ample opportunities for a view beyond the local scene. Dr. Paul Westerberg, the pastor during my adolescent years, was himself a powerful preacher and teacher. Then, too, we would be visited by leaders in the global Lutheran community. One memorable visitor was Bishop Bo Giertz of the Diocese of Gothenburg, Sweden. He spoke in our church in the spring of 1953 when I was but fourteen years of age and soon to experience the Rite of Confirmation. To this day I have one of the bishop's works, a brief booklet titled *Liturgy and Spiritual Awakening*,[16] it probably having been available during his visit. The booklet's very title reminds me of my father. While he had indeed experienced a spiritual awakening some years earlier and in a setting other than Lutheran, he remained faithful to the Lutheran tradition and its expressive, some might say elaborate, liturgy. Dad was present to hear Bishop Bo Giertz.

The influence of those encounters on Dad's world view had to have been profound. Although he wasn't much given to expressing at length whatever thoughts or feelings such luminaries engendered within him, that he was affected there is no doubt—affected not only in his own sense of humility having been reinforced, but also in his quiet appreciation of the world beyond the sphere of his daily routine. Indeed, perhaps it was the combination of an innate humility and an inner expansion of his world view that recently prompted earlier quoted Karl Mattson, when reflecting on childhood memories of my father, to say that he "had an aura about him," and that he, Karl, "always felt safe around him." How appropriate, when spoken of one who was in the healing business.

Certainly a venue contrasting both amphitheater and church nave is a public setting hosting the Ice Capades. On an evening in the mid-1950s and due to the thoughtfulness of my Uncle Art and Aunt Gladys, Mom and Dad were taken to Buffalo for entertainment they otherwise had little access to. In fact, I'm uncertain whether they'd ever attended a performance of such a dramatic display of skill sets as those displayed on ice. From Dad's perspective alone, when measured against those of a hospital corridor, a patient's room, or emergency and surgical suites, what he was witnessing in that arena had to have been a wonderful momentary distraction. But then it was no less so for Mom, who daily ministered to her elderly and ailing mother. I suspect that both of my parents were, as the saying goes, in another world as their senses absorbed sights and sounds so unfamiliar.

Rockefeller, Niemoeller, Bo Giertz; on occasion, and compared to the usual, an extraordinary display of athletic and entertainment abilities. And Dad's response? He would have been amazed at the variety of commitments represented in what he heard and saw and, not least of all, grateful for the resultant sharing of gifts on the part of others.

CHAPTER 15

———◆◆◆———

The Oldest of Eight—
the Quieter of Two

The home in which I was raised was matriarchal in nature. Aside from whatever personality traits both Mom and Dad brought into their marriage, Dad being at work thirteen out of every fourteen days in all the years of his hospital employment certainly contributed to, if not determined, the family dynamics at home. It was simply the reality that the parent who was present most of the time was in the day-to-day, situation-after-situation, decision-making role. Also, the reality of my ailing maternal grandmother being part of the mix for nine crucial years—eight of which were those immediately prior to my leaving for college—added to Mom's responsibilities and therefore to her often decisive words and actions.

Then, too, there was the fact of Dad's relative quietness. That is, his demeanor was that of the gentle, soft-spoken person he was. Not that my mother was not gentle or was lacking a soft-spoken side. Rather, she was more the openly in-charge person in the family than Dad. The instances when she might have said, "We'll decide that when your father gets home," they are too few to recall. And to the extent that Dad had grown up in a matriarchal setting, which he may well have, contributed to the *modus operandi* in his marriage.

How Dad, having been raised in a family of ten and being the oldest of eight children, was influenced in who he became is a question not fully to be answered. Indeed, contemporary discussion of oldest and middle child syndrome theories is itself not conclusive due to disagreement among professionals in the field. However, the discussion began a century or so ago: "Alfred Adler (1870–1937), an Austrian psychiatrist, and a contemporary of Sigmund Freud and Carl Jung, was one of the first theorists to suggest that birth order influences personality. He argued that birth order can leave an indelible impression on an individual's style of life, which is one's habitual way of dealing with the tasks of friendship, love, and work. According to Adler, firstborns are 'dethroned' when a second child comes along, and this may have a lasting influence on them."[17]

My dad's personal history includes the second of the Carlson children, Carl, having died in infancy. While he didn't much verbally dwell on that loss, he did once speak of "my baby brother" and with me briefly searched for his gravesite. And as for dethronement, of his other six siblings, two were girls and four were boys. So yes, surely a kind of dethronement might have been experienced on Dad's part. From the necessity of a mother's attentiveness alone, to what extent must that diminish once the next sibling, and the next, and then the next comes along? To an only child such as I, being one, let alone the first one, among that many is obviously quite outside anything in my experience.

In addition, something of a mystery piece contributed to Dad's earliest years and his becoming the person I came to know. Soon into the beginning of his third decade and for some thirteen months, Dad was a patient in a nearby hospital known to area residents for its treatment of mental disorders. He who one day would be my father was diagnosed with a condition that in recent decades, and in terms of contemporary usage, has disappeared from the psychiatric lexicon.

It turned out to be a brief chapter in Dad's young adult life, one that in later years was barely mentioned. In fact, at this point in time I don't recall ever having discussed it with him. Probably it was Mom who mentioned it. But because it was never an issue in our family's life, it was truly a matter of what had passed.

Something else I also learned from Mom was that, on occasion during Dad's early years, a neighbor family, the Sandbergs, would take him to their farm located a distance outside of the city. They would do so, Mom said, to remove him momentarily from the family setting. But for whose benefit primarily—for Dad's, or for the rest of the family? And were such removals prior to his hospitalization or afterward? I've never had the impression that Dad, because of his age, in any way dominated among his siblings. Indeed, the opposite has been my impression. I can imagine that, because of an innate reticence, he may have been, even in his youth, on the quiet side and thus the object of others' not ill-intentioned teasing.

Both Mom and Dad were the oldest child in their family of origin, Mom being the oldest of two. Perhaps her matriarchal nature stemmed in part from that fact, whereas the characteristics that Dad brought into their marriage were in large part informed by having grown up, by comparison, in a crowd.

Although I was not present, I can imagine how a conversation between my parents and the congregation's pastor sounded, literally. Over the years, Mom had issues with Pastor Westerberg, as I'm certain he had with her. Eventually, feelings on Mom's part reached the point where the pastor was invited to the house, the intention probably being to clear the air, as it were. Later, Mom shared with me that, at some point during the visit, the pastor said, "No one has ever spoken to me this way." I add with emphasis that my relationship with Pastor Westerberg, my confirmation pastor, was always a cordial one, he having been my sponsor at ordination, and then several times in the ensuing years having invited me to preach in my home church.

But back to the conversation that was to have cleared the air. I'm certain the pastor's blunt observation was not intended as a compliment. And, from my parents' side, I'm equally certain that my mother had done most of the talking, Dad perhaps occasionally signaling a vocal assent. It wasn't that he would have disagreed with what his spouse was saying to the pastor, or that he was anything but in agreement with her most of the time and on any subject, from politics to religion. Rather, and especially in such a situation as here described, he was the quieter of the two. By contrast, usually my mother spoke what she was thinking. Such was the case when a neighbor lady, herself elderly as was Mom, expressed envy following one of my visits home. Said she, "Oh, how I wish I had a child who would come to visit me!" And to the childless woman Mom replied, "It's a little late to think about that, Mildred."

All of this is not to suggest that Dad was not a social person. That he in fact was a social person is evident many times when reading his diary entries during the early years of his retirement. There were numerous and purposeful encounters with people: volunteering in the therapy department in the hospital from which he had retired; visits in both of the city's hospitals and in nursing homes to provide personal care to male patients referred by their physicians; and visiting in private homes simply, I'm sure, for the sake of conversation.

While often in Mom's presence Dad would be the quieter of the two, but whatever that might have projected, it was far from the whole picture. My cousin, Elaine, recently wrote of her uncle: "I remember that your dad did a lot of visiting. He was always thinking of others. He was a very kind and compassionate man."

Yes, my father was the oldest of eight and the quieter of two. But of most importance is this—his own testimony in the early months of his retirement from his diary dated January 12, 1967: "My dear wife and I are going down to the retirement home this morning, doing volunteer work. We just love it, helping others when we can." I still have the badge Dad wore when at the retirement home—LSS Volunteer, it says. And this from an entry nine days later, on the 21st: "Thank God for one whole year of retirement ... of health and happiness with my dear wife."

All of which seems summarized in a 27-by-19-inch color print by British artist, Daniel Sherrin, that hangs framed over my desk. It is titled: "Where Time Has Brought Peace and Contentment." Handwriting other than Dad's on the back of the print reads "Property of J. Chandler Carlson, 114 William Street, Jamestown, N.Y." And it is dated November 2, 1936.

Then, on Thanksgiving Day of that year, Chandler Carlson and Ruby Haskell were engaged, their wedding to occur a mere six months into the future. But whence the picture—from whom, or from where? I remember Dad speaking of it as something he brought into the marriage, and during all of my formative years, it hung over the buffet in the dining room, both on Charles Street and later on Willow Avenue. Finally, it hung over the same piece of furniture when on Aldren Avenue.

Artist Sherrin being British, the painting depicts a peaceful English village, a shepherd and his dog walking behind a dozen sheep, thatched-roof dwellings on either side of the dirt road, and a church building with its prominent steeple in the background. Was Dad drawn more to the picture itself, or perhaps to its title, highlighting time, peace, and contentment? To what extent, too, might its attraction have been Dad's awareness of the name Chandler having English roots?

Given what was transpiring in his life at the time and, not least of all, the years that had passed preceding that moment, my hunch is that the artist's work was beautifully symbolic and the title precisely nailing Dad's thoughts and feelings, with 1936 nearing its end, and the approaching year holding so much promise.

CHAPTER 16

---•◆•---

"Like an Angel's Dance"

On May 18, 2014, our nephew, David Holstius, received his PhD from the School of Public Health, University of California, Berkeley. Environmental health science being his interest, David's dissertation title, "Monitoring Particulate Matter with Commodity Hardware," reflected that focus.

The commencement address was given by Dr. Anthony Iton, MD, JD, MPH, senior vice president for Healthy Communities at The California Endowment. He highlighted three necessary elements that contribute to pursuing a fulfilling vocational journey: *passion, gifts*—as in personal attributes that support the passion—and *career*, i.e., a more than short-term commitment to the focus of one's passion.[18]

Not only would my father's six years of elementary education never have resulted in a dissertation such as nephew David has contributed, but there is considerable doubt that Dad was ever aware of a vocational triad such as described by Dr. Iton. And yet his commitment to what indeed was his career included each of the three necessary elements. I know that because I had the opportunity to work with him.

What preceded her comment, I don't recall, but I was twenty-five feet down the corridor when the evening supervisor called out to me, "If you turn out to be half as good as your father, you'll be all right."

It was the summer of 1960, and I was filling in as an orderly for those on vacation. Dad had worked at the hospital for thirty years.[19] I knew he was held in high regard because I had heard so much already in my still young life. Although cliché, the nurse's words were meant for me to take to heart. And now, here I was, like Dad, in white attire and working alongside him. I believe that, for Dad, the only time other than during his hospital working hours he would dress in white was still four years away when Faith and I would marry. How very elegant in appearance he was during those evening hours of September 5, 1964, in Pleasantville, New York, dressed in his white jacket and black trousers.

The atmosphere of the hospital had long been familiar to me. Our home on Charles Street being only a short walk to the hospital, as a young boy I'd sometimes meet Dad when his shift ended. Waiting in the orderly room, I would see the lockers, hear one orderly report to another, and became accustomed to hospital sounds and odors. It was in large measure what gave me the impetus, years later when in college and seminary, to get part-time work as an orderly in hospitals located in St. Paul, Minnesota, and Moline, Illinois, as well as in Jamestown. Those brief early ventures into Dad's working domain made, what for so many people remains space to be avoided, for me space in which I grew to be comfortable.

Easily recalled is an incident from my early childhood. Mom and I were walking to the downtown area, the walk taking us past the lower end of the sizeable hospital grounds. As we neared the end of Barrett Avenue, there, across the street and off to our left some twenty-five yards, were Dad, another hospital employee, and a patient. Later, we would learn that the patient had wandered out of the hospital—itself some distance up the hill—and now Dad and his coworker were attempting to persuade the patient to return to the space he had been assigned. It was an unusual sight and occurrence. And it was for me an early look at the nature of my father's work: tending to a patient's needs, sometimes necessitating even a walk out-of-doors. Search and rescue comes to mind.

What I had heard time and again down through the years was how much Dad's encounters with people who had been patients at the hospital meant to them. Such testimony had not come from Dad himself. Instead, I heard the comments from the former patients themselves or, just as frequently, from a member of a patient's extended family—when on the street, on the bus, in downtown stores, in church. These comments were spoken most often either directly to Dad or, in his absence, to Mom. What was there about this plain man that inspired such gratefulness?

There were few people on the hospital staff and of whatever rank who were paged on the intercom more than Dad during his daily eight-hour shift. Whether to assist in lifting a patient, set up an oxygen tent, transport a patient to or from surgery, or to do any number of other things an orderly was called upon to do, a nurse, a physician, or a patient could count on one thing, always, in Dad's response: a willing, competent, and encouraging presence.

To be sure, that would have been expected of anyone in Dad's position. But in my father's case there was a consistent, daily, moment-by-moment empathy for the patients that underlay all of his bedside encounters. I am convinced that it was not the technical duties he fulfilled that made his presence memorable, but rather the nontechnical, unasked for ministrations that elicited the gratefulness. Dad always noticed, for example, when a patient's head had slipped down on a pillow. And he would take the few seconds necessary to make the adjustment, assuring the patient's greater comfort. The late Jennie Vimmerstedt, writing in the July 29, 1961, edition of Jamestown's *Post-Journal*, testified as follows:

> To thousands, who through the years have been patients at Jamestown General Hospital, Chandler Carlson is more than an orderly. Now in his 30th year

on the hospital staff, he has become an institution, not only among his associates who have the highest regard and admiration for him, but also among patients he has served. For when hospital experiences almost have been forgotten with time, patients still remember a kind, tender person with a brotherly concern over how they felt and what he could do to make them more comfortable. They remember how often they heard his name called for countless tasks, and his quick cheerful response, and how each day, in spite of the many duties he had to perform, he stopped by their bedside to fluff up their pillows and leave a quiet greeting.[20]

Dad's hands, I believe, transmitted healing—not the healing that comes with technical ability such as in a surgeon's hands, but the kind of healing that is innate and conveyed with compassion. I remember as a young child having a headache that had not dissipated by bedtime. Dad was then working the evening shift, and I said to my mother, "When Dad gets home, be sure he comes in and puts his hand on my forehead." Although I was too young to have the word *compassion* in my vocabulary, I knew the effect of my father's hands. Is it not possible that more than a few patients did as well?

As much as anything else that motivated Dad in his vocation was the force of the words *service above self*, a phrase I heard on June 28, 2014, while with my son and seventeen-year-old grandson during an orientation visit to the United States Coast Guard Academy in New London, Connecticut. Seamus, himself to be a senior in high school three months following that visit, was interested in hearing what life as a cadet in that service would be like and in what directions it might one day lead.

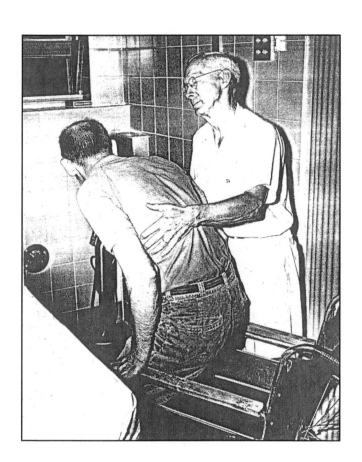

Service above self—while Dad himself may never have heard the phrase, I heard it several times during the hour-long session in New London, and it accurately describes what my father believed, what drove him, and what his interactions with people, especially with patients, revealed about him.

For all of his caring as expressed toward others, he also cared about his own physical well-being and, in the pursuit of good health, may have been something of a pioneer. Some years into his retirement and a long time ago given the scope and number of present-day medical advances, Dad was already daily using a self-prescribed medication as a prophylactic. Or was it as a palliative? Whatever was the case, he had come to have confidence in an item named Empirin Compound, an aspirinlike tablet that was available over-the-counter. I was unfamiliar at the time, as I think were most people, with the idea of taking a medication for anything other than relief of existing symptoms, and occasionally I would question Dad about his expectations. "Do you really think that taking an Empirin every day helps you?"[21] Today we are told that low-dose aspirin, when taken on a regular basis, can reduce the risk of heart attack, colorectal cancer, and stroke. Depending on his motivation, my father may have been on the cutting edge of medicine's responsiveness.

Dad came in contact with all sorts of human condition and misery in his thirty-six years at the hospital. He would not betray confidences or even talk much about his daily routine. What I most often heard him say was, "If you have your health, you have everything," and *that* he would affirm with fervor, probably not realizing that he was echoing "The first wealth is health."[22] It can be argued, of course, that it isn't true—that health isn't everything—that without friends, or without a sense of purpose and individual worth, health alone can leave one pretty empty. Dad, I think, would not have denied the power of the argument. However, given the tenure and focus of his work, neither is he to be denied the power of his oft-spoken dictum.

A colleague of mine once observed of patients in a sizeable New England hospital, "There's more thinking per square inch that goes on in that place than anywhere else in the city." That was the milieu in which Dad worked and out of which he spoke. Rightly or wrongly, he *assumed* friends, purpose, and a sense of self-worth. He also knew that, even with those ingredients in place, diminished health was less than life was meant to be. Thus, in those holy moments of bedside presence, when a patient's thinking would necessarily bow to a prescribed procedure, and Dad's assuring and encouraging words would combine with his gentle touch, diminution would give way to peace and no doubt sometimes even to hope.

Recollection does not bring back ever having heard my father speak of a connection, yet one has to wonder to what extent the thirteen months of hospitalization during his still young life prompted his later choice of work in a hospital setting. While at first his work there was only during winter months due to the lack of work in the family sheet metal business, the day came when the hospital insisted he work full time year-round. Instead of looking for other winter work, he exited John Carlson & Sons in favor of assisting in the work of healing human bodies, not sealing together inanimate pieces of metal. How could that decision, that choice, not have had something to do with his own earlier hospitalization and, as his sister, Adeline, once noted, himself having been made well?

The first of Dad's given names, Joseph, although hardly ever appearing other than simply as the letter J, highlighted the essence of his vocation. In the Genesis story of Joseph and his brothers that comes to an emotional climax in chapter 45, the writer records, "He said, 'I am your brother, Joseph, whom you sold into Egypt. And now do not be distressed, or angry with yourselves, because you sold me here; for God sent me before you to preserve life'" (Gen. 45:4b–5 NRSV). My father, Joseph Chandler Carlson, assisted physicians, nurses, technicians, and others in making people well, i.e., in work no less significant than that of preserving life.

Passion, gifts, career—those words, while not appearing above except in the second paragraph that begins this chapter, are woven into the fabric of this story. My dad lived what Theodore Roosevelt highlighted when he said, "Far and away the best prize that life offers is the chance to work hard at work worth doing."[23]

Dr. James Nestingen, professor emeritus of Church History, Luther Seminary, St. Paul, Minnesota, when speaking of grace, has described it as that which "moves so softly, so quietly, so gently, like an angel's dance, moving across the day and which we hardly recognize."[24] Dad in his work moved that way, and it is good that in his own time so many of his contemporaries recognized it. However, the truth is that Dad would be the last to claim for himself any angelic attributes, certainly not in any innate sense. He would have understood the apostle's words to the Corinthians: that while he had behaved "with frankness and godly sincerity," such behavior was motivated "not by earthly wisdom but by the grace of God" (2 Cor. 1:12 NRSV).

Upon Dad's retirement, Mom wrote the following in a diarylike reflection: "No, Chandler is not going to let the rocking chair get him. He plans to still give of himself. He will be a blessing in the lives of people just as long as he lives. He will always be known, as he is known throughout our city, as 'an angel of mercy.'"

CHAPTER 17

---•◆•---

Having a Leg Up

The incident here recalled is a perfect illustration of the truth highlighted by Charles Dickens as conveyed on January 12, 2015, in *Real Simple* magazine's "Daily Thought" via the Internet: "There is nothing in the world so irresistibly contagious as laughter and good humor."

Gales of laughter didn't often emanate from Dad. Maybe it was his nature, fed by a mixture of Nordic reticence and seriousness. And it wasn't that he was humorless. He knew the lighter side of life, occasionally bringing home anecdotes from the hospital that highlighted the vulnerability of human pretense.

In fact, it was at the hospital where Dad himself was a key player in an incident that in later years would cause him to laugh almost uncontrollably whenever the incident was mentioned.

It was simple enough and innocent enough as well. Dad was picking up soiled linen that had been put into large laundry bags and then depositing the bags into a laundry cart. On one of the floors where he'd stopped for the pickup, a nurse had positioned herself next to the pile of bags, apparently her white apparel from toe to head blending in with Dad's target. Being in a hurry as often was the case, he reached down and, in wrapping his arms around several of the bulging receptacles, he included one of the unsuspecting nurse's legs in the manual hoist. How many seconds that inadvertent grab lasted is unknown, but I can imagine the noisy and instantaneous reaction of the nurse. Who was more startled—the orderly or the nurse, the grabber or she who was grabbed?

Human nature all but assures that my father's embarrassment had to have been at high pitch for several days, maybe even for weeks, as the incident made its way through the hospital staff grapevine. "Have you heard what Chandler's been up to?" and similar questions no doubt served as prelude to the story.

If such a thing happened in today's sensitive workplace environment, one might be accused of sexual harassment. But sixty-five years or more ago some workers would have used the incident only to titillate the imagination as to the laundry bag-and-leg-grabber's carnal intent, thereby playing on Dad's already manifest embarrassment.

That embarrassment prominently came to the fore even decades later whenever Dad would be asked, either by me or by one of his grandchildren, "Tell us again—*what* happened that time with you and the laundry ...?" Even we could not resist occasionally tapping into the laughter promised by that singular moment of Dad's inattentiveness.

"Well," he would begin hesitantly, "I was collecting the laundry, and ..." Usually, that concluded his recitation. His hand would come up to his mouth as if to contain what he knew was coming, and laughter would momentarily take control of him. He might try to finish the sentence, but almost always it was to no avail. And we would laugh too, of course. It wasn't necessary for him to finish what he had begun, because we all knew what was to follow.

In spite of my dad's almost daily contact with the bodies of men and women alike—often, especially with males, in very personal ways—to whatever extent otherwise the carnal was part of his consciousness, he kept it all to himself. He wasn't a storyteller, let alone those of a ribald nature. He was human though, and it happened that life's delightful mixture, in which sometimes hints of the ridiculous and the sublime comingle, came together in Dad's always predictable response to an increasingly long-ago incident that combined innocence, a suggestion of the carnal, gross embarrassment, and, not least of all in ensuing years, occasional moments of laughter within the family.

CHAPTER 18

Manipulation Preferred

At first it seemed like a near disaster. In fact, that's an apt description. Dad had been retired barely a year when a fall from a ladder severely injured his left shoulder. The telephone call came on the evening of February 27, 1968. Mom told Faith and me that Dad was in the hospital, having been outside earlier in the day and, against her expressed wishes, sawing off branches from the spruce trees that bordered the property on the corner of Willow Avenue and George Street.

Removing the dead lower branches from the elegantly tall white spruce planted by my maternal grandfather decades earlier was an ongoing project and one that Dad enjoyed. On this day, his daughter-in-law's twenty-fifth birthday, he apparently decided to celebrate by being out in the fresh air. With Mom going downtown to do some errands, what was to prevent him from getting a little exercise? She'd be none the wiser, he must have thought.

Neither ladders nor height intimidated Dad. He had often climbed when working with his father in the sheet metal business, installing new eaves and downspouts on houses. He'd even been out on the high, steep, and treacherous slate roof of the church building on

Chandler Street, secured by a rope, when his father's business had been contracted to tend to necessary maintenance on that sharply slanted and foreboding slope. The trouble was that, on this day, the frozen ground was unreceptive to the angle of Dad's ladder. By the time Mom arrived home, Dad had been sitting on the frigid ground for nearly three hours, propped up against a tree. The pain and shock from the seven-foot fall had all but immobilized him.

What happened next tells much about my father's character and his approach to people. Once at the hospital where he himself was so well-known, he had a choice of three orthopedic surgeons: Drs. Childress, Nelson, or Curran. The first two were well-known and respected by the entire medical staff, their combined practices in the city already having totaled many years. By contrast, not having been in the community very long, Dr. Curran was a less familiar presence. However, because Dad felt that choosing either one of the other two physicians would result in hurt feelings of the one not chosen, he turned to Dr. Curran.

Word reached us that several of the surgical nurses who over the years had come to know and respect Dad weren't pleased with his decision. They felt he'd be best served by going with a better known quantity. They would have been even less enthused had Dr. Curran's remark to Dad after having viewed the X-rays, as later conveyed by Mom, gotten back to them. "Well, Chandler," he said, "I don't know what I'm going to do with you. You've crushed it."

Instead of opting for an invasive procedure in which he'd attempt to reconstruct the shoulder with the inclusion of pins, Dr. Curran decided in favor of manipulation. Dad was taken to surgery, given a general anesthetic, and, by viewing intermittent X-ray images, the physician manipulated the shoulder pieces back to as near normal placement as possible.

There followed a seven-week stay in the hospital, during which time Dad's shoulder was kept in traction. He was now beginning his seventy-second year, but there was no hint of the pneumonia that some feared would develop from his extended exposure to winter's ground.

One of the physicians tending to him—involving a minor procedure unrelated to the shoulder—presented no bill. Dad thanked him, probably more than once, to which the physician responded, "Really, Chandler! After all *you've* done for people?" Well, yes. How could any physician who frequented the hospital not have known what that physician knew?

As spring turned into summer and Dad was asked how he and "that left shoulder" were coming along, he always answered, "I can do what's necessary." Dad was left-handed. But imagine being in an extreme situation, one requiring the most informed medical judgment possible and then choosing a physician chiefly to avoid offending either one of two others. Yet that so characterized Dad's attitude toward people. In midwinter 1968, it was an attitude that served him well. For much of the rest of his life, his left shoulder was useable and relatively pain-free.

CHAPTER 19

---·•◦•·---

Who Was That Masked Man ... and the Fellow Wearing Plaid?

The identity of the masked man on the hospital staff at the Jamestown General was well known to most employees, especially if the months were August, September and to the fall day that would result in the first significant frost. In his middle years Dad suffered from hay fever, suffered not being too strong a word. It was especially egregious after 1949 when we moved to Willow Avenue, the property being adjacent to ragweed- and goldenrod-laden fields.

At home during the nighttime hours, lying down gave way to sitting in a chair, for that was the only way Dad could adequately breathe. While at work, so as not to be tending continuously to the attention his nose required, he wore a surgical mask inside of which he placed a piece of absorbent gauze. That was best both for him and for the patients alike.

Thankfully, as Dad lived further into his senior years, and either because of improved medications, the aging process itself, or both, the annual and often harsh symptoms of this seasonal affliction diminished. But yet another mask was to come into play, one he would use in a very different public setting. That mask, too, would assist him in allaying a major nasal aggravation.

Finally, it was the smoking that persuaded him. Initially, Mom and Dad traveled to New England by bus from western New York to Rhode Island to visit our family during our early years in New England. Even with the nearly seventeen-hour trip, the duration was mitigated somewhat by the picturesque sights along the way: the fieldstone walls outlining much of the countryside, the New England town greens with their white clapboard churches lighted during the early evening hours, the occasional stop when passengers got off the bus for a much-needed break.

For the same reason that so many other people avoided air travel, Dad refused to fly. "I'll fly as long as I can keep one foot on the ground," he often said. Then one day he announced to Mom, "I've had all I can take of long bus rides and smoke. The next time we visit Dan and Faith, I think we should go by plane."

Mom wasn't entirely surprised. In fact, she'd been anxious during the previous couple of bus trips when Dad, in an effort to filter out at least some of the cigarette smoke hanging like a pall inside the vehicle, donned a large handkerchief—really, a colorful bandanna that covered much of his face. He looked, she said, like a bandit and, with the increasing number of hijackings occurring among various modes of public transportation, the fear of her husband possibly being misread by someone was understandable.

In the late spring of 1968, my parents began using air travel. The man who much earlier in life had fallen backward off a horse-drawn wagon was now a full participant in the age of flight. While smoking was still permitted on planes, the trip took much less time. And, of course, Dad could leave his mask at home.

His use of masks was not the only occasional attire that distinguished my father. In August 1969, our young family went camping in western New York, in the Gowanda area, where we met the Hunter family, Tom Hunter being a seminary classmate and by then serving a Lutheran congregation in Kentucky. Our son, Curtis, was two years of age, and our daughter-to-be barely in utero—a discovery awaiting us in a crowded Beirut, Lebanon, airport the following month.

Dad, however, was seventy-two, Mom, sixty-one, and neither had any camping experience in their bios. That they agreed to join us for an overnight—it may have been for two nights—remains a bit of a surprise. It is most likely that they were simply glad to be invited, to be included.

Our camping accommodations centered on a 1964 Nimrod pop-up trailer, a welcome and literal step up from the earlier twelve-by-sixteen-foot tent, the Nimrod having been purchased from its original owners the previous year. It was in excellent condition, but still, the novice and older campers would be sleeping on an extended tray, restroom facilities being a distance from the camping site. Happily, with all of it the grandparents adjusted quickly and well.

Among the memories of that brief multigenerational encounter with the out-of-doors, an image that stands out is one that presented itself at Letchworth State Park. Known as the Grand Canyon of the East, it was a reasonable drive's distance from where we were camping and a stunning gift of nature none of us had previously visited. So off we went. Would the experience itself match our expectations?

One might think that the image standing out all these years later would be a photograph of Letchworth's magnificent gorge or of one of the park's three major waterfalls. But no, it is of something quite different, namely a photo of Dad on a hiking trail and dressed in plaid, i.e., in plaid cotton shorts and a plaid shirt, the two plaids not matching. Although, come to think of it, perhaps the image would have been even more striking and memorable if the plaids had matched.

In any case, the image was not, nor is it, the material for a men's clothing ad in *Esquire*. But then requirements for such were not high on the day's agenda. The man who wore hospital whites much of the time, in-the-garden work clothes several times each week especially from June into October, and his Sunday best every other week, on this day was a camper, sightseeing with his family in the surroundings of a national treasure. His clothing coordinates were not foremost in mind.

To be sure, what my dad wore in any setting was not what defined him. Clearly, on the occasion here recalled, his plaids were evidence of his having taken to heart the First Century rabbi who advised, "do not worry about ... what you will wear ..." (Matt. 6:25 NRSV).

CHAPTER 20

High above the Mist

I recall as a boy hearing of Dad, prior to his marriage, having been in Milwaukee, Wisconsin, for a brief time. Yet from 1937 on and given family budgetary constraints, one might have thought that travel much beyond the Chautauqua County area itself would have been lacking. And while there wasn't much by way of my parents traveling purely for their own enjoyment, some traveling there was.

Besides the trip to eastern New York State in 1946, Mom and Dad attended my graduation from Luther Jr. College, Wahoo, Nebraska, in 1959, as well as my graduation from Augsburg College, Minneapolis, Minnesota, in 1961, and later from the Lutheran School of Theology at Chicago, Rock Island Campus, Rock Island, Illinois, in 1965. They also traveled to Evanston, Illinois, during my year of internship, 1963–64, and in early September of 1964 to White Plains, New York, when Faith and I married.

Then there was the trip in the 1970s to Greenville, North Carolina, to visit Faith's parents, Elvin and Eleanor Holstius. Having first come to our home, at the time in New Britain, Connecticut, they traveled with our family, by then including our growing children, Curtis and Carolyn; the three generations traveling together was to make the time on the road all the more enjoyable. A highlight of that trip was sightseeing in the nation's capital—an opportunity I suspect that neither Mom nor Dad had much entertained ever would occur.

A memorable moment of the Washington visit involved the fire alarm at the motel where we stayed before going on to North Carolina. Sounding in the middle of the night, neither of my parents awakened. So much for sleeping lightly.

Most memorable, however, was a day trip to Niagara Falls, Ontario, Canada. Faith, the children, and I were visiting Jamestown in the late 1970s. While the falls had been a stop on our honeymoon some thirteen years earlier, the experience awaited the children. Taking Grandma and Grandpa with us would add to the excitement.

Once there, it was the four youngest of the group of six who chose to descend the forebodingly steep rail ride to the Maid of the Mist, the oldest two watching from above. And when the ride of legend ended, it was time to get something to eat.

Why not, we thought, try the restaurant we'd read about—the circular, revolving restaurant high atop a spindlelike structure. It was but a half mile or so distance from our present location, so we set out on foot for the 775-foot high Skylon Tower. Oh, how much fun it would be!

Whether it was actually approaching the restaurant's closing time or, more likely, that we were trying to take advantage of lower prices prior to evening servings, our pace was not what one would term indolent. If Dad was at all familiar with the term sprint, he might well have been thinking, *This must be what that is.* Clearly, we were walking beyond what his comfort zone would normally permit. Yes, his diary of those years indicates that a daily walk in the neighborhood was not unusual. But at a let's-get-there-before-it's-too-late pace? Definitely not. Nor was it our intention that Grandpa's spleen be unduly challenged by a race to cuisine. Had anyone observing us knew of our destination and also was aware of the epicure's conclusion that "gastronomy governs the whole life of man,"[25] they might have thought, *Well, there goes living, fast-walking proof.*

Did Dad protest? If so, only mildly, although he may have been wishing that the earlier misty ride had been delayed in its return and thus possibly having avoided the present hasty exercise.

In the end, a major physical setback was somehow avoided. We arrived at our destination, our hearts beating a bit faster than usual, to be sure. And once at the tower's top, it was the lovely and impressive setting that we had anticipated. We inquired of Dad just how he was feeling, he quietly assuring us that all was well. While eating, however, it would have been understandable had he silently been giving thanks that he was present—present not only to see the view and enjoy a meal—but present at all!

A few years later when again visiting in Jamestown, our family experienced the impact of what appears to have been aging even on a person who for so many years was as active as was my father and as evidenced in the following chapter. Barely a five-minute drive from the apartment were two or three fast-food restaurants, one of which we had in mind at lunch time. But Dad clearly did not want to leave the apartment. He was as adamant about it as about anything I remember him addressing at that moment in his life. However, the grandchildren, Faith, and I encouraged him and ultimately we prevailed. Into the van the six of us went.

Once in a booth and having placed our orders, Dad seemed no worse for the brief ride, even though, as I recall, on that occasion we were not at Kentucky Fried Chicken, the dietary offerings of which both he and Mom thoroughly enjoyed.

Still, I wonder at what seems to me now as insensitivity, not least of all on my part, to Dad's reluctance to leave the apartment that day. While neither he nor Mom identified anything in particular that would have hindered him physically, clearly something prompted his reluctance. Whatever its source, it is equally clear that the earlier Niagara Falls trip—with its impromptu energetic walk to the towering eatery—was taken none too soon.

CHAPTER 21

───◆◆◆───

The Healer's Therapy

On a February 4 in the late 1970s, the congregation's pastor, Pastor Westerberg, telephoned to wish Dad a happy birthday. "Is Chandler there?" he asked. "Not right now," Mom replied. "He's in the garden." Parsnips, as any gardener knows, are best harvested at midwinter.

It had been a stressful time in early 1949 when we moved from Charles Street to Willow Avenue, the home of my maternal grandparents and the place where my mother had lived before her marriage. Mom's parents and their two daughters were the original occupants, my grandparents having had the house built, taking occupancy in 1927. Now Grandma Haskell, Anna, was blind and had been living alone since Grandpa's death seven months earlier.

The passing of the months had its salving effect, however, and gradually we settled into routine. There were the several flower gardens to reclaim after months of inattention, a project that fell to Mom herself. Dad reclaimed the vegetable garden bordered on three sides by the towering white spruce. It was an interest he would avidly pursue for some thirty-five years, until he was in his mideighties. I marvel at it now, not because he gardened as an elderly man, but because some twenty-five years earlier when neighbors, men years younger than he, were permanently turning their gardens under because they were too weary to tend them after a day's work, Dad kept at his gardening. All those years, during winter's waning weeks, he would peruse seed catalogs in boyish anticipation of what to plant come spring. A diary entry dated February 26, 1982, reads: "I am just waiting for planting time to come."

By the day of Pastor Westerberg's birthday telephone call and as a later chapter will reveal, my parents had moved once again, the destination being the nearby Lutheran Social Services retirement community. It had been a timely move in early 1974, especially for Dad, who not many months before had noted in his diary one instance in particular when his nephew, Tom, had assisted with a major project in the Willow Avenue house. It's also worthy to note that, in contrast to some senior people who move from the very familiar to the unfamiliar—initially questioning their decision, or worse—I'm not aware that either Mom or Dad ever looked back. Besides having had such a move in mind for a number of years, the house they were leaving was less than three miles from the new apartment to which they were going. And for Dad in particular, the opportunity to continue his gardening undoubtedly helped make the new setting not only acceptable, but a destination to be glad about as well.

The two grandchildren, Curtis and Carolyn, always looked forward to summertime visits, especially during the later years as they became more aware of the delight their grandfather found in the produce of the earth. "Grandpa, may we see your garden?" they would ask, always knowing what the answer would be.

Dad's gardening was not only his hobby, but his therapy as well. In contrast to his work in the hospital, where with rare exception everything he did was in response to a request or order, gardening was just the opposite. In the process and pattern of gardening, nearly everything except nature's forces was *his* call. And then there was the soil; he loved to work the soil, turning it over every spring, preparing the individual repositories for the seeds, cultivating the rows with his hand-powered cultivator, even the weeding. Today, the same cultivator that contributed to Dad's garden flourishing is used by his grandson, Curtis, and great-grandsons, Seamus and Jacob, at their home in coastal Maine.

Oh, and how much Dad enjoyed sharing the results of his gardening! There are numerous entries in his diary, not least of all in his later years, of harvesting one item or another—from parsnips in February to varieties of vegetables in September—and giving them to neighbors and relatives. In fact, he would pack shoe boxes with parsnips and mail them to relatives from California to New England. Just such an instance is recorded in this note from him, one dated March 9, 1977, during our last spring in New Britain, Connecticut:

Dear Dan & Faith,

I am sending you some of our parsnips this morning. Give some to Pastor Gustafson if you don't like them, or to someone else who does like them. Mother has gone down to Gladys this morning for a Tupperware party. I thought it would be fun to do this now, so you could taste them anyways. We have a beautiful morning here—sun shining, spring in the air. I can't wait to dig in the garden. May these few lines find you and your family well. With God's blessings. With love, Dad

When I was a child, I believed that my father had no major interest such as other boys' fathers, interests such as fishing, hunting, or golf. But I was wrong. This man, who all my formative years and longer worked alternatingly forty-eight and sixty-hour weeks, working thirteen out of every fourteen days with only every other Sunday off, kept his garden going during those years and then for some eighteen years into retirement. And it was for the most part a solitary, uninterrupted activity, quite the opposite of his work at the hospital, most at-home vegetable gardens not being equipped with intercoms.

"Grandpa, may we see your garden?" asked the grandchildren, and with a smile, their grandpa would answer, "Sure, let's go have a look."

CHAPTER 22

---•◦•---

The Greatest Wealth Possible

In the years of my childhood, I became aware of having peers whose family financial circumstances were far different than mine. It was a fact of which I was reminded not least of all on Sundays while at worship.

Specifically, two families in our congregation were owners in industry. The Marvin Peterson family, and also Marvin's sister, Alberta Morse, were members of the church. Their father, Karl Peterson, had founded the Crescent Tool Company. Marvin and his family would regularly sit two or three rows ahead of where our family sat during worship. And the Hugo Lindgren family regularly sat one or two rows behind where we sat. Hugo, an immigrant from Sweden, had founded Jamestown Metal Products.

Contrary to dwelling on the disparity between what an owner in industry had in annual income compared to that of a hospital orderly, conversation in our home centered rather on our being fellow Lutherans and members of the same congregation. I'm fairly certain that, when I was a very young child, both Marvin's and Hugo's wives, as was my mother, were members of the Cradle Roll group at church— mothers and their children who would meet for fellowship probably on a monthly basis. Years later, Marilyn, a daughter of the Petersons, and I were in the same confirmation class. And the Lindgren twins, Richard and Robert, and I were in church choirs and in youth group and, in high school, were in both the marching and concert bands as well as the a cappella choir.

Also as a teenager, I was in both the Peterson and Lindgren homes. When in the former, at its Lakewood location, the occasion was an open house. I can still hear Mr. Peterson, when guests were being shown his at-home den, say with a chuckle, "This is where the lion roars." Being at the Lindgren home, located at the far end of Beechview Avenue in Jamestown, was when the church's youth group had a sledding and toboggan party in a nearby field.

Both families have been responsible for enhancing the work of Lutheran Social Services (LSS)—today locally known simply as *Lutheran*—in Jamestown on its main campus and what my parents called home during their later years. For example, the chapel on campus, Christ Chapel, benefits from Morse funds, while funds from the Karl Peterson Trust are annually designated for the Lutheran Home. The Lindgren family saw to the building of the Lindgren Apartments, several two-story, eight-apartment buildings designed as independent living space for retired individuals and couples. Mr. Lindgren, it was said, wanted senior folk in town to have access to comfortable and affordable housing during their more vulnerable years. Very happily, Mom and Dad lived in one of those apartments beginning early in 1974. By the time of my mother's death in 2002 and between the two of them, they resided on that campus a total of forty-three years.

Earlier, in the summer of 1958, Mr. Lindgren's accessibility and generosity were demonstrated to me personally. It was my first summer home from college, and I learned that a youth group to which I had belonged had disbanded, leaving a three hundred dollar debt at a local radio station. For a number of years, the group had recorded a fifteen-minute devotional program that was aired on Sunday mornings, time for which the group paid. Because of my involvement with the group,

I was determined that the debt be eliminated. With the help of my mother in identifying potential donors, I approached a number of individuals face to face, asking for their assistance.

After hearing my account of the need, one well-known industrialist responded by saying, "I've been asked to give to a lot of things over the years, but never to a dead horse." And with that he turned away. By exemplary contrast, Mr. Lindgren came out of his office, listened to my brief story, and then handed me a fifty dollar bill. In my eyes, that was a large contribution toward a fairly modest goal.

As the years progressed, the friendship between the Lindgrens and my parents was nurtured. A contributing factor was the Lindgrens' decision themselves to reside in one of the apartments on campus, one located across the street from Mom and Dad. They lived there for several years, until moving permanently to their Florida home in Ft. Myers. Also, Mom was involved annually in raising funds among LSS campus residents on behalf of the on-campus ministry to children, namely the Gustavus Adolphus Children's Home, by then having been present for many years. Indeed, it was the initial ministry on campus and remains there to this day. Mom's effort on its behalf was a project in which Mr. Lindgren took an interest.

Regarding the Lindgrens and Florida, early in the 1960s Hugo himself was hugely instrumental in the decisions that resulted in the construction of the now familiar causeway connecting Sanibel Island to the mainland. That saga is reviewed in an article titled, "The Shy Caesar of Sanibel" written by the late Al Burt, a well-known Florida columnist and journalist.

Hugo and Louise Lindgren were present at my father's funeral on August 23, 1989. I remember briefly speaking with them at the service's conclusion. What strikes me at this point in time is the reality of the greatest wealth possible in this life—that of friendship— having been shared in their later years between these four aging and long-time Jamestown residents. I recall my parents saying that, during the winter months when the Lindgrens would be in Florida, Hugo would telephone them, inquiring how they were doing. And consider the following from Dad's diary:

> July 3, 1982 — "Ruby and I are going over to celebrate Hugo and Louise's 45th Anniversary."

> September 26, 1982 — "Hugo and Louise are coming in for a cup of coffee this afternoon."

> June 11, 1983 — "Hugo and Louise are taking us out for lunch at Holiday Inn."

> September 25, 1983 — "We are having Hugo and Louise in for a meal this evening."

> August 9, 1984 — "Hugo stopped by for a visit."

What an affirmation of friendship as the greatest wealth possible! The man whose industry in 1948 provided metal cabinets for the remodeled White House kitchen, the hospital orderly, and their wives—friends.

CHAPTER 23

---·◆·---

Forgiveness: Given or Received?

The one who forgives gains the victory.[26]

Dad once said of an incident that had hurt both Mom and him deeply, "I have forgiven, but I'll never forget."

Still, he was always inclined to forgive, an inclination that led him to view himself as the possible recipient of another's forgiveness. He himself shared with me that, when a younger brother lay dying, he said to his brother, "If I've ever said or done anything to offend you, I ask your forgiveness." The brother, whose condition by then prohibited him from speaking, motioned by hand as if to say, "Never mind, it isn't necessary."

Dad's sister, Adeline, recalls him sitting at the kitchen table and, in response to someone commenting negatively about an acquaintance or neighbor, he would say, "Just look at yourself and don't criticize other people."

Besides it being so characteristic of Dad, I've sometimes wondered what lay beneath the deathbed exchange with his dying brother. Was there something in the recesses of Dad's memory, something he may once have said, done, or felt, that he needed to assuage in the little time that remained? While that is possible, my understanding of his boyhood family history was always that the brother, more than Dad himself, may well have had reason to ask forgiveness. Dad may have been the oldest among the siblings, but he was not the most inclined toward self-assertion. He was not given in his adulthood to cutting others down nor, I suspect, in his childhood to playing on others' weaknesses as frequently children do.

What is more central to Christian faith—love or forgiveness? Not that they're unrelated. And at what age does a child begin to distinguish between the two, or understand their connection? It would seem that, in my father's case, growing up in a home as one of seven children with a seventeen-year span between the oldest and the youngest would provide ample opportunity to learn, indeed to practice, something of each. In my own life, and whenever it was that I began assimilating the essential place of both love and forgiveness in the life of faith, what I am most aware of, now halfway through my eighth decade, is that practicing either is never a matter of doing what comes naturally. Essentially, either characteristic of attitude or behavior, and of which I'm ever an example, occurs only with the Spirit's prompting.

Whatever in their lives prompted the final communication between Dad and his younger brother, peace was proffered there at the hospital bedside. And, as the brother's life neared its end, the wave of the hand was a kind of absolution, blessing, and farewell all at once, only the two brothers knowing what lay beneath the silent gesture.

But then, no one else needed to know.

CHAPTER 24

———— ·•·•· ————

The Surfacing of a Divergent View

The home in which I was raised was dry. That is, alcoholic
beverages of any variety were absent. Indeed, prohibited is not
too strong a word.

That absence derived from two sources, the first of which was a
certain piety. Yes, the gospel writer records Jesus as having provided
a considerable amount of wine for the wedding at Cana, and the
earthly elements in the Eucharist include wine, and Martin Luther's
affection for beer is a fact of record. Although Luther is also credited
with having said that while beer is a human product, wine is divine.
In honesty, my parents likely were unaware of Luther's drinking
preferences. Very simply, their piety eschewed alcohol as part of one's
diet.

The second source was a case of alcohol-related illness on the
maternal side of my mother's family. Grandma Haskell had a brother
who died an early death due in part to his consumption of alcoholic
beverages. He was otherwise an able and productive person. Mom
shared with me that her uncle was one of the best typesetters

Jamestown had in the early 1900s—that, if something went wrong with the printing process at the city's only newspaper, he was the one called upon for his expertise. Mom was born in 1908, two years before her uncle's death at age thirty-seven.

Thus, piety and family history kept alcohol out of my boyhood home. The same, however, was not the case in my wife's childhood home. In fact, it's a bit of that family's history that my mother-in-law's father, himself a pious immigrant Swede and Lutheran pastor, in his senior years began drinking modest amounts of red wine, although for medicinal purpose it was to be understood. No doubt Gustav Knut Andeen, G.K. as he both referred to himself and was known by others, was aware of the encouragement provided in Scripture itself: "No longer drink only water, but take a little wine for the sake of your stomach and your frequent ailments" (1 Tim. 5:23 NRSV). As a point of interest, the late Peter J. Gomes, beginning in 1974 minister in The Memorial Church, Harvard University, wrote of what the Bible says about drink,[27] i.e., alcoholic beverages.

Upon leaving home for college in 1957, I did not immediately make a dash for that which till then I had been denied. Far from it. And at this point in my life, never having acquired a taste for beer, plus my judgment of a fine wine settling for a well-known and sweet Concord grape variety, well, that pretty much indicates my level both of knowledge and of interest in drinks alcoholic. In fact, given my once near addiction to soda, I've been heard to say of my preference in wine, "It's a lot like soda except that it lacks the carbonation."

At one point in the mid-1980s, my wife and I invited colleagues and their spouses to our home for an evening of conversation and refreshments. We did so on a number of occasions, given my role as dean of Boston area congregations. In announcing the occasion here related, Faith had put together a colorful and attractive invitation, one that included the common BYOB notation. In fact, it was so attractive that I decided to mail one to Mom and Dad, thinking they would appreciate it. In retrospect, how little I really was thinking!

Once the item was in the mail and I realized that someone would interpret BYOB for my parents, the anticipated reaction was soon heard. For some time we had been communicating by cassette tape. Instead of a weekly letter, we would listen to the others' voices. In this instance, the first tape to arrive after receipt of the invitation conveyed surprise, disappointment, and chagrin; all were among the feelings expressed. And I responded, of course. I spoke with both clarity and passion regarding my own piety and maturity, noting that, by then, I had probably lived half my life and that I was capable of making the appropriate decisions.

The next tape to arrive from home began with Mom saying: "Dear, dear, dear Dan ... in the months before you were born, I carried you right under my heart ..." I don't recall what followed that except Mom quoting Dad as having said, "We've done all that we can for Dan." As noted in an earlier chapter, Mom was the primary spokesperson. But at the time I understood Dad to be saying that, yes, Dan must be left to make his own decisions in these matters.

After my response to their initial reaction a week earlier, might my father have initiated a heart-to-heart with my mother? Considering what had preceded that moment, including a hint or two from me in preceding years that perhaps their views on the subject were not now mine, I am struck by the realism and fairness in Dad's statement. His comment was meant as much for his wife's benefit, I think, as it was a letting go of his son.

The issue did present itself a year or two later during a Christmas Eve dinner in our Arlington home, in which setting again we offered wine. Dad had died four months earlier, but Mom was present. One guest who was present, that year's intern, noted with conviction, "After all, Jesus drank wine!"

It is just as well, no doubt, that neither of my parents is present for the recent practice of some congregations that encourages, indeed schedules, conversation on matters of faith as well as the singing of hymns in locations associated with, well, with drinking. For example, God on Tap is the label given such an opportunity in one location, the setting announced as "a place for conversations that happen at the intersection of life and faith." Clearly, part of the motivation that underlies the practice is the hope of engaging individuals whose lives are not intentionally faith-oriented.

Current practice being what it is, while I am not aware if Mom ever did modify her view on the matter, it wasn't discussed further. Nor did Dad, except through Mom on the aforementioned tape, ever raise the subject with me after having become aware of the BYOB invitation. And, even had the family budget permitted the occasional inclusion of items alcoholic, whether knowledge of research indicating that alcoholism is more likely generated in homes where the beverage is totally absent than where it is moderately in use would have made any difference in my parents' judgment on the subject is highly unlikely. Why? Because a deeply ingrained piety combined with a broader familial culture is a greater force.

In the end and as for how the subject most recently affected my relationship with my parents, it's as a Prairie Home Companion character might say: It could have been a lot worse. Thankfully!

CHAPTER 25

---·•·---

What a Friend!

During my parents' latter years, I made the trip home from New England to western New York every three to four months. As I once wrote in the parish newsletter of St. Paul Church, Arlington, Massachusetts, being the only child and in terms of our nuclear family, if this child didn't visit my parents, no child would visit them. At some point in the last twenty-four months of Dad's life, it must have seemed to him that the length of time between the last visit and the next was longer than usual. He said to Mom, "Isn't it about time for our friend to visit?"

Our friend? At first Mom really did not understand to whom he referred. "Friend?" she probably responded, and of course Dad clarified just who he had in mind. Mom shared that with me, and I'm uncertain whether it struck her as more humorous than unusual. But I've remembered, and it causes me to ponder my relationship with my father as friend.

The word *friend* is interesting in itself. For example, the practice of sending annual letters at year's end is known to many of us both as senders of same and as recipients. How often the salutation reads, "Dear Family and Friends." Certainly we know the meaning of family and also that it's possible to be closer emotionally to some friends than to individual members of one's family, whether the latter be of the immediate family or extended. Also, on occasion a person is heard to say, often during a period when there is an issue causing tension between parent and child, "I don't want to be her friend; I want to be her parent."

When a young boy, I'd sometimes hear Dad speak of his friend, Elmer. How close in age his friend was to Dad I'm not aware, but I do know that he owned a grocery store close to the Carlson William Street home. Indeed, it may have been Elmer who was the motivation for Dad spending some time in Milwaukee, as I seem to recall hearing that it was he Dad had followed there. Likewise, it may have been his grocery delivery wagon from which Dad once fell, an incident mentioned in an earlier chapter. I believe it was before Dad married that friend Elmer died. He remains the only person from Dad's early years with whom I ever heard Dad claim friendship. "My friend, Elmer," he would say.

In marriage, Dad and Mom had a number of friends outside of the family itself. Yet of the two of them, Mom perhaps had the closest friend. She and Margaret Johnson became friends while in grade school, and Margaret as a young girl contracted what one public health nurse judged to have been "the worst case of polio that Jamestown has ever had." Margaret, however, survived, was seriously handicapped all of her remaining years—she lived well into her upper middle years—and Mom regularly visited her until her death. Even though confined to a wheelchair and assisted with her breathing by an upper body brace, Margaret was able to function in the kitchen, preparing meals. And she took up painting. A lovely oil painting, a winter scene showing several skaters on an icy pond that she gave to Mom, is now displayed in our home.

To my knowledge Dad had no one with whom he had bonded in such a friendship, although his friendship with Elmer may well have been of that quality. Not that he was friendless otherwise, of course. There were the many visits he made on individuals in hospitals and homes, not least of all in his retirement years. And both he and Mom were befriended nearly countless times over the decades, especially during the 1970s and '80s, by a number of people who offered them rides to one place and another, such as to church and home again on a Sunday morning.

But I return to the earlier question: From whence did my father's reference to me as friend come? Did he simply misspeak? Might there have been a deep-seated and, except for this instance, unspoken need or hope for friendship with his son that had gone unmet? Or, *was* I in fact as much friend as I was a son to him?

In the mid-1970s I took a course in Transactional Analysis, otherwise known as TA. At some point during a group discussion, I remember expressing anxiety that, for all of my Dad's longevity and mine, in the end I might never really have gotten to know my father. At the time of that comment, Dad was to live some fifteen more years, living to the age of ninety-two and a half. Although in my own vocation I was absent from the home many evenings when our children were in their formative years—a fact of which I am acutely aware today—and when a teenager myself I was absent of an evening more than was Dad, still his thirteen out of every fourteen-day work cycle was noticeable. We did not have a lot of personal time together. Seldom did we have deep personal conversations.

Added to that is an incident that took place when my parents were visiting our family in New Britain, Connecticut. Dad and I were outside, briefly talking about yard work and lawn care. He mentioned something he had recently read or heard about the subject, and I quickly dismissed it. His response was a quiet no, his tone indicating resignation to my opinion. Why wasn't I open to hearing more, to listening? It's a disturbing memory. To paraphrase Joseph Sittler, quoted in an ensuing chapter, it's amazing what the human brain is capable both of retaining and of resurfacing throughout a lifetime, sometimes, as in this instance, to our discomfort.

I pray that my father never felt his son did not regard him with respect and gratefulness. At one point in their later years he and

Mom received a letter from me, a letter in which I expressed my appreciation for each one's gifts to my life, saying that I would always remember my mother for her sense of rectitude and my father for his compassion.

If Dad, in saying "Isn't it about time for our friend to visit?" was, consciously or not, revealing his view of our relationship, I can only express gratitude. And it is with certainty that he and I shared a confidence in the words of him into whose life, death, and resurrection each was baptized: "I do not call you servants any longer, because the servant does not know what the master is doing; but I have called you friends, because I have made known to you everything that I have heard from my Father" (John 15:15 NRSV).

It well follows that a hymn with which Dad grew to be very familiar is titled "What a Friend We Have in Jesus," two lines of which read, "Do your friends despise, forsake you? Take it to the Lord in prayer. In his arms he'll take and shield you; you will find a solace there."[28] Dad in his lifetime did have friends, the principal one of whom remains faithful to him even now.

CHAPTER 26

While Waiting

The Lord is good to those who wait for
him, to the soul that seeks him.
—Lamentations 3:25 (NRSV)

Consider the occasions in a lifetime that, at least in part, can be captured in the word *waiting*. They are numerous, such occasions are, and they vary widely in the range of human experience.

Perhaps classic is the waiting that young children go through in anticipation of the celebration of Christmas. How often a child is heard to say, "I can't wait until Christmas is here!" Yet wait she does, and he does, and they all do. And while waiting? There is the hoping that the gifts received will match what has been suggested or requested.

The child's very presence recalls the waiting that brought the child into the world in the first place. Pregnancy—both parents-to-be wait, to be sure. But who would not agree with the mother that her waiting is extraordinarily special, a waiting that the father cannot fully appreciate? Given that without her waiting there would be no birth, well, the point is made. And while waiting? On the part of each parent-to-be there is the hoping that the birthing will proceed without complications and that the newborn will be healthy.

Then, too, in most cases, there is first the waiting of the romantic relationship that precedes, to use traditional language, two becoming one. "Does she feel about me the way I feel about her?" And vice versa. Or, "Dare we make such a momentous commitment in a time when the breakup of marriages seems so prevalent?" Quite a number of years ago, a prospective bride, just days before the wedding, came to me privately, questioning the course about to be taken because, as she said, "Another person's life is nothing to tinker with." Then, not long ago, that bride's mother assured me, thankfully, that the couple remains together. And while waiting for the wedding bells to ring? There is the hoping that a relationship begun in and with promise will mature and, in a word, endure.

Waiting. How about waiting for the physician's telephone call, advising of the lab test results, especially when suspicions of trouble run high already? Or, in these increasingly hazardous days, waiting for the call from a loved one assuring that, yes, the plane has safely landed, or the road travelers reached the destination.

During my days as a seminary student, Dr. N. LeRoy Norquist once said to our class when suggesting we be attentive to a particular segment of a course of study, giving it some concentrated attention, "Much can be accomplished while waiting for the wife." He said it in his usual quiet, undramatic way, which somehow, in that instance, added to its force. Enough among us were married to understand the import of his humor-intended comment. If only humor had underlain Dad's experience in 1986 when he had an unusual moment waiting for my mother.

It was a Wednesday, October 29, to be exact, the day during the week when Mom and her sister, Gladys, went to the mall. By 1986, Aunt Gladys had pretty much stopped driving, public transportation having become their means of maintaining their weekly social time together. And it was a pleasant ride from the LSS campus where Gladys, too, now resided, the ride taking them the several miles from one side of Jamestown to the mall in Lakewood, immediately beyond the other side of the city. The sisters would do some shopping, have lunch, and then return home.

That was the usual pattern. On this day, however, their return trip made an unexpected stop. Not far from the mall itself, but inside the city limits, the bus and an errant automobile collided. The two shoppers, Mom and her sister, were seated in the back seat of the bus—apparently a space they had come to prefer—and with nothing directly in front of where Mom was seated, the impact threw her several feet down the aisle. Her most obvious physical injury was a deep laceration on her right shin, requiring an immediate trip to the Jamestown General Hospital, as that was closest to the site of the accident.

At the time hospital procedures on my mother began, or certainly shortly thereafter, was about the time the sisters would otherwise have returned home, each to their own apartment on the LSS campus. And of course, not being aware of what had happened on the other side of town, Dad was expecting Mom home in the hour that he was accustomed to her return.

Mom's own diary states that she was in the hospital emergency room from 2:45 until 9:00 p.m. Having no immediate word from anyone as to what had taken place, it's not a wonder that Dad's diary shares little information, reading simply, "A very dark day with rain. Ruby is out shopping with Gladys. In accident." Some days later and once things had settled down a bit, Mom told me that, during those several unscheduled hours of her absence and of Dad's anxious waiting, he sat on the modest bench they kept in the hallway, outside the door into their apartment. He sat there, looking out the window, waiting. He might just as well have remained in the apartment itself, it having ample views to the outside world and from two directions. The bench in the hallway was chosen perhaps because it was closest to where Mom would first be welcomed home.

And while waiting? It is difficult for me to imagine what Dad was going through emotionally as Mom's arrival was one, then two, then three, four, and more hours late. What was *he* imagining? He who depended on my mother for so much, might he have been imagining life without her? How could that possibility not to some extent have added to the confusion, to the mystery, to the high anxiety of that fading fall day? If there was any consolation at all, it had to have been in the context of prayer. Or might he have been too anxious for that recourse to have been engaged?

My dad, who sixty-eight years earlier had waited thirteen months before being released from a psychiatric hospital; who had waited forty years before marrying; who waited year after year for seeds he had planted to take root and produce what he so enjoyed harvesting; who indeed believed "The Lord is good to those who wait for him"; he—now well into his ninetieth year—was experiencing a wait the likes of which he hadn't before known. And the relief he must have felt when his dear wife again appeared is as difficult to imagine as the helplessness he must have felt in her unexplained absence.

Mom's injury from having been thrown down onto the aisle floor of the bus would take several months to heal—in fact, five. The deep wound, near to the bone and what contact with the aisle floor might have brought into the tissue being unknown, was left open. Healing would take place, literally, from the inside out. Treatment at home, under supervision, was mainly the daily application of saline soaks.

As for Dad: Whether a sound medical assessment or not, Mom herself believed that the strenuous waiting episode that he had gone through ultimately contributed to the physical crisis with which he was to be confronted only two months later.

CHAPTER 27

———•:•◦•:•———

Yes, Everyone

The first word of his illness came on Christmas Day 1986. Dad was then just a little over a month away from his ninetieth birthday. In his diary for that year, the writing ceases on the 11th of December.

"I've been better, Dan," he answered when I phoned with Christmas greetings and to hear how he and Mom were doing.

The next day he entered the hospital—the same hospital he had labored in for thirty-six years. He remained there for several weeks before being transferred to a nursing facility on the Lutheran Social Services campus, the same campus where my parents resided. By the time I arrived a couple of days later, a diagnosis had been confirmed.

"Your father is a very sick man," said the urologist. "He has uremia."

Yet Dad would survive and live two and a half more years. But those days between Christmas and early into January were tenuous. Each evening when Mom and I returned from the hospital to the apartment, we didn't know whether there would be another visit.

On one of those wintry evenings so common to western New York, I went out to run an errand and had a chance conversation with a longtime acquaintance of our family. The fellow apartment dweller, knowing that Mom and I were making daily trips back and forth to the hospital, said with emotion, "Everyone loves your dad."

It sounded so right, so undeniable, his declaration: "*Everyone* loves your dad." But was it possible that my father had no enemies, or at least no detractors? Besides, this was twenty years into his retirement. Hardly anyone presently employed at the hospital remembered him. Scores of people he'd served, and served with, over the years were no longer living. Were those the neighbor referred to still so populous that they could be identified as "everyone?" How frequently one hears on media talk shows someone say in reference to a current event— often one of minor significance—*Everyone is talking about*, when in reality and given the nation's three hundred million people, hardly anyone is talking about the identified subject.

Certainly part of the *everyone* could be attributed to both Mom and Dad early into retirement's years having volunteered at the LSS senior living facilities, sometimes referred to in Dad's diary as "the home." Besides housing dedicated to independent living, LSS provided, and still does, both assisted living and skilled nursing services.

For his part, and as his diary frequently attests, a particular service that Dad had honed over the years, providing shaves for male patients, was continued. "I went over to the home to shave some of the men," says his entry on April 19, 1975, just one year into living on the campus. In addition and no doubt at a physician's request, he would go to a private home to change a patient's Foley catheter. For such services as especially the latter, Dad was sometimes given a modest payment, what today would be regarded as pocket change. Strictly volunteer or not, however, I am certain his primary motivation was the patient contact.

The testimony of that neighbor had been on the mark. The man my father was that Christmas week, his ninetieth birthday only five weeks ahead, was essentially the same man the community had come to know over a span of nearly four decades, both in the city-owned hospital and, prior to that, as the oldest of eight children born to John and Christine. His quiet and gentle demeanor, his lack of pretense, his transparent caring for others, the joy he got out of sharing—not least of all vegetables from his garden—nearly all of it remained intact to the end. It had sounded so right, so undeniable, because everyone who had known my father over the years, however few they now numbered, did love him.

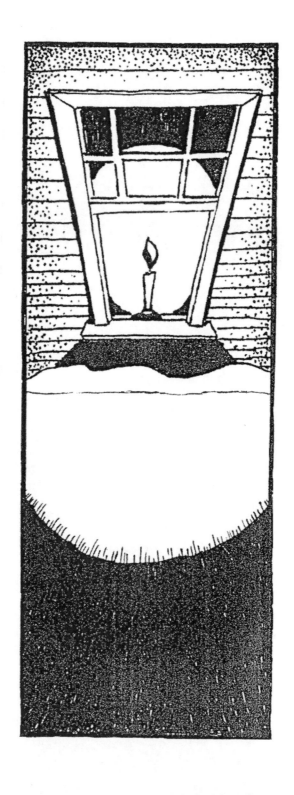

CHAPTER 28

<hr/>

In the Candle's Glow

It was not unusual for me to drive past the old house on Charles Street during visits home, the house having been in other owners' hands nearly thirty-eight years when I drove by on that January evening. It was the New Year's second day, 1987, and I was on my way back to the hospital where Dad's life continued to hang in the balance. Instinctively, I stopped the car just to look and to remember. The scene was familiar yet somehow surrealistic, a street-level front window's orange bulb seasonal candle casting its glow on the newly fallen snow. How assuring it was that the owners of recent years had taken care of the place. And how different it must have looked on this night compared to its appearance when Mom and Dad first looked at it!

Memories filtered through my mind: winter's thick frost on the window of what had been my unheated bedroom; the old maple tree out front, now long gone, the aboveground roots of which used to provide after-rain miniature pools; my dad installing the new eaves and downspouts; how during the war years—World War II— he would leave in the middle of the night for the hospital, an upper arm displaying the Civil Defense emblem, responding to an air raid alert; how large the Christmas tree used to look in the bay window, a window that lent so much character to the living room, indeed, to the house.

But most of all on this night I remembered how, on a winter afternoon when I was frustrated by a backyard that was not sloped enough to provide a downhill experience even for an eight-year-old skier, Dad, upon arriving home from work, took shovel in hand and built a snowy mound down which to ski. Although the imagery had been softened by time, through memory's mists I recalled that it happened and knew that I could not possibly have been as grateful then as I was now.

At that moment, in that place, the earth seemed hushed, and the warm glow of the illuminated snow in early winter's coldness eased my mind back to the present, and to the hospital, and to the stark reality of the ebb of life that awaits each one of us.

CHAPTER 29

<hr>

36 ~ at 50 ~ in '87

When I was an adolescent, a group of youth of which I was a part had as an occasional participant a fellow early into adulthood. He was good-looking, drove a Kaiser-Frazer car, might have been a chaperone among us (but wasn't), and not least in importance was an engaging personality. Some of his peers annoyed him when insisting that he demonstrate some seriousness about moving on with his life, as in getting married. In mentioning his annoyance to us, he memorably said, "I will not marry as a punishment for growing up."

Our friend eventually did marry. The last I remember seeing him easily goes back some twenty years. It was on a Sunday morning when visiting my home congregation and assisting in distributing the sacrament; I can still see him and his wife kneeling among the communicants.

<hr>

Except for the fact that, as the twenty-first century continues, fiftieth wedding anniversaries may be less and less in evidence, what can be said about such an event that's of interest to anyone except to the particular family in which the occasion presents itself? In my parents' case, however, the celebration almost did not occur. The diagnosis as 1987 began and as previously noted was not conducive to hope brimming over. Given the physician's brief and stark summary to me regarding Dad's condition, even survival for the short term was questionable. And yet as May approached, and thanks to Mom's knack at organizing, plans for a celebration advanced.

The setting was to be at the Marvin House, a once venerable dwelling more recently become a place of modest community gatherings, on the corner of Main and Fifth Streets. And in the end, not only was it to be, but it was—the hoped for celebration happening on May 30, 1987. When Faith, Curtis, Carolyn, and I arrived, Mom and Dad and also one of Dad's nurses were already on the scene. What my father had been through in the preceding five months was somewhat evident in his appearance, e.g., his posture in the wheelchair being slightly bowed.

Mom, though, had seen to his being dressed as appropriately as she, his loosely knotted tie likely being designed for his comfort's sake. Mom with her corsage and Dad with his boutonniere were ready to greet their guests.

Almost startlingly, a total of thirty-six individuals were present. And the distances they traveled ranged from North Carolina in the south to Toronto in the north, and from Massachusetts in the east to California in the west. In fact, just the previous month the honorees' daughter-in-law, Faith, had returned from Eastern Europe and Russia following a month-long trip with a dozen other women of the Lutheran Church in America, having visited women active in the church's mission from East Germany and Poland to Moscow and Leningrad (now, again, Saint Petersburg).

Seated with Mom and Dad at the head table were Mom's sister, Gladys, who had been the matron of honor at the wedding, and also Dad's tending nurse from the Hultquist Infirmary on the LSS campus. Others in attendance included each of Dad's surviving siblings: his brother, Philip, and his wife, Jean, from Jamestown itself; his brother, Oscar, and his wife, Dorothy, from Nebraska; and his sisters, Adeline and Hildur, both from California. In addition, one nephew and five nieces were present, four of them accompanied by family of their own. Absent were Dad's three deceased brothers: infant Carl, Augard, and Levern.

Besides the obvious motivation of wanting to celebrate the anniversary, the motivation otherwise was, principally, simply to be together. Of course, there was a lovely luncheon. How often food is essential in fostering both celebration and communication! Granddaughter Carolyn sang a solo titled, "To Me" by Mack David and Mike Reid. Both she and grandson Curtis served as the table hosts among their peers. Mom made a few remarks of welcome and gratitude, with Dad, the quieter of the two, seconding her sentiments, and then saying, "God bless you all." But those traditional, anticipated pieces of the event were secondary to, again, the honor given my mother and father simply by the presence of those who had responded to the invitation from near and far.

Now, nearly three decades later and in a time when marriages enduring five decades appear less likely an expectation, what, I wonder, was in the mind and heart of each during the family gathering, i.e., of the two who fifty years earlier had become one?

For Dad especially, who was already forty years of age when, with his eleven years-younger bride, vows were exchanged, what must he have been thinking, feeling, indeed believing about life and relationships? Answers to such a question must be left to speculation; his diary cannot be consulted, entries therein having ceased six months earlier. However, it is all but certain that dominating whatever else he was pondering on that remarkable day, overwhelming gratitude in assuring, soothing, wavelike repetition flowed through his gentle spirit and over his physically struggling body. And that their son and daughter-in-law celebrated their fiftieth year as husband and wife in 2014 would be a joy to both Mom and Dad today.

Marriage—a punishment for having grown up? Not when you had reached the beginning of your fifth decade as had that bachelor at 114 William Street. Instead, over the years, by both words and actions, Dad affirmed what the biblical writer notes: "He who finds a wife finds a good thing, and obtains favor from the Lord" (Prov. 18:22 NRSV).

Father and son, reflecting on the day's memorable event.

CHAPTER 30

The Mind and Nearly Last Things

Those of steadfast mind you keep in peace—
in peace because they trust in you.
—Isaiah 26:3 (NRSV)

Assuming that near the end of life a person's mental acumen remains fairly well intact, what an array of memories presents itself from and on which to ponder—some welcome, others no doubt troubling. What capacity has the human brain! As noted the late theologian and author Joseph A. Sittler: "There is something in the associational, in what we call the infinite retrievability of the past. It is embedded in the senses, in the chemistry, in the cerebrum somehow; it makes computers look simple."[29]

That reads as something from another century, as indeed it is, having been published in 1981. And although it's from as recent a century as the twentieth, advances in technology are happening so fast that unimaginable, if not downright scary, projections are not uncommon today. Consider: a weekly news magazine recently had as its cover title, "Can Google Solve DEATH?" It was subtitled, "The search giant is launching a venture to extend the human life span. That would be crazy—if it weren't Google."[30]

Writing at an earlier date, Lev Grossman wrote of the Singularity movement, or transformation, as in artificial intelligence (AI), that has its roots in the work of Raymond Kurzweil. If Kurzweil's projections become reality, then, writes Grossman, "We're approaching a moment when computers will become intelligent, and not just intelligent but more intelligent than humans. When that happens, humanity— our bodies, our minds, our civilization—will be completely and irreversibly transformed. He believes that this moment is not only inevitable but imminent. According to his calculations, the end of human civilization as we know it is about thirty-five years away."[31]

In fact, are there not signs of Kurzweil's projection being well along in its manifestation? How else to interpret the numbers of young people, and some older as well, who are all but inseparable from their iPhones, a wire dangling from their ears as they move through their daily activities—a rapidly growing dependence on that technical apparatus, a dependence that begs the question of who or what is in control. Whatever anxiety the present reality may generate in some observers, and in spite of physicist Stephen Hawking's and private spaceflight pioneer Elon Musk's dire predictions regarding AI's ultimate effect on human civilization,[32] Kurzweil remains optimistic, providing there is a continuing advance of, what he terms, "our social ideals."

But back to Sittler of 1981 and to my father in the latter months of 1988. I recall sitting with Dad in a day room at the LSS nursing home during one of my visits home; it was a year before his death. While his hearing was impaired and his eyesight gone, his mind remained lucid. And on this particular day he was reflecting back to his years when a much younger man at home, the years prior to his marriage at least five to six decades earlier.

His exact train of thought as expressed audibly I do not recall— not to mention not knowing whether he spoke of all that his mind was processing—but what I did hear was a reflection on what he had contributed to the household, something about his mother, and then the words, "I was only trying to help." He said it as if to be saying, "I wish she'd understood." Indeed, Mom in her legacy notes records that, when she and Dad married, "He didn't have anything. He would spend his whole paycheck for groceries. He was carrying an insurance policy on his father. He bought a new truck for the business. He was sure he would never get married and he could always, if necessary, go to the Poor House in Dewittville."

"Only trying to help." Might Dad's mother, out of an understandable pride, protested if her eldest child had applied personal income to family expenses? In reality, was it his father who was speaking through his mother? Or perhaps he brought home unsolicited items that he thought would contribute but of which my grandmother did not approve.

Whatever the case, remembering his youngest sister's testimony of her eldest brother not having a selfish bone in him, I also recall having been told by my mother that, when the sister was in high school, a friend once complimented her on a dress. To which the sister responded, "I wouldn't have this dress were it not for my brother, Chandler."

Although even today too few people ever get around to executing an estate plan, i.e., to having a will, certainly those who do have a will have seriously considered last things. Mom and Dad each had a will. But on that day some twenty-six years ago, when visiting with Dad in the nursing home day room, his mind, in connecting decades-old family dynamics with present feelings, was dealing with *nearly* last things, with that of which his senses, his cerebrum, and for whatever reasons would not let go.

Once, in those latter days of his physical decline, Dad said to me, "Dan, we wear out!" Indeed we do, and probably no two of us experiencing precisely the same gradations of decline in either mental or physical abilities.

At the moment here recalled, what was the nature of the dynamics

Dad's mind had stored, and what exactly was he feeling? To my regret all these years later, I did not probe enough to learn more. And now I'll never know. My comfort lies in the knowledge that, in his depths and true to the prophet's words, my father's spirit was at peace because of his trust in the Lord God.

CHAPTER 31

What Was He Looking At?

Dad's work schedule during the thirty-six years at the hospital limited his church-going to every other Sunday. The setting was the church building, located on aptly-named Chandler Street, in which he had been confirmed and married. His baptism, I believe, occurred at home, that practice not being unusual in the latter nineteenth century.

As were Dad's parents, the congregation was made up largely of Swedish immigrants and their immediate descendants. And, from the nave that seated in excess of one thousand people to the majestic altar in the chancel—one that held, and does to this day, three statues, the largest and center statue being Thorvaldsen's Christus—not to mention the historic liturgy based on that of the Church of Sweden, those were reasons enough for some Swedish believers, but themselves not Lutheran, sometimes to speak of Lutherans as "Catholics in disguise."

Dad, however, had another side. That is, while being faithful to the Lutheran tradition, he at the same time appreciated other expressions of the faith. For example, on Sunday mornings while preparing to go to church, often the radio at home would be tuned to The Old Fashioned

Revival Hour broadcast from Long Beach, California, with Baptist preacher Charles E. Fuller holding forth. I think Dad appreciated Fuller's preaching which, really, was similar—similar in the sense of fervor—to what one would hear from Walter A. Maier later in the day on the Lutheran Hour originating from St. Louis, Missouri.

Also, there was the music, typified, for example, by the male quartet's singing of "This world is not my home I'm just a passing through. My treasurers are laid up somewhere beyond the blue ..."[33] Dad himself wasn't much of a singer. But he could carry a tune, always giving it a worthy try when at worship. I remember him once expressing his appreciation for the hymn "Jerusalem, My Happy Home," the text being in reference to the life to come. And references in his diary to him and Mom going to sing-a-long gatherings on campus during their LSS years were frequent.

In the context of the Sunday morning broadcast from Long Beach, I've always felt that between Fuller's preaching and the quartet's singing, Dad was taken back to the experience years earlier when hearing the Swedish evangelist at the Salvation Army—that he was reminded of a singular and deep spiritual moment in his life.

Indeed, it was the depth of his faith that permitted him during his final three years, so beset by illness, to accept them as a test rather than as an unwarranted burden. How familiar Dad was with the name Dietrich Bonhoeffer, the German Lutheran pastor, theologian, and dissident anti-Nazi, I do not know. But of Bonhoeffer contemporary writer Jim Belcher shares the following: "In March 1938, he preached a sermon titled 'The Secret of Suffering' based on Romans 1:1–5. After the events of 1937, he saw suffering not as something to avoid but as a gift. He did not believe that suffering was ultimately a good. But he saw that God could use it for good. Bonhoeffer told his audience that God often uses suffering to try and test our faith, making sure it will be strong enough to stand on the last day."[34]

Once, while in the LSS nursing facility, Dad said to Mom, "We are being tested." Bonhoeffer and my father were born on the same day but nine years apart, February 4—the pastor in 1906, he being the younger of the two.

Just as on that increasingly long-ago evening Dad had *gained* a sight that prior to then he hadn't had, very near the end of his life his physical sight suddenly *ceased.* He was blind. Yet even as his earthly world darkened, the sight most precious to him was retained. In fact, on the day of his death, and as Mom stood at his bedside, Dad, as he lay there, kept looking up, his eyes fixed on a ceiling corner in the room. His gaze upward was noticeable enough that an attending nurse asked, "What are you looking at, Chandler?"

Yes, just what *was* he looking at? The sight that was still very much active, an inner sight, is best summed up in still another hymn. The final stanza of "Be Thou My Vision" reads: Light of my soul, after victory won,

> may I reach heaven's joys, O heaven's Sun!
> Heart of my own heart, whatever befall,
> still be my vision, O Ruler of all.[35]

That was my father's faith, his anticipation.

CHAPTER 32

---•◦•---

Artificial Grass Neither Required nor Desired

Virtually all of the graveside services I have attended over the years have been scenes where carpets of artificial grass have covered the temporarily piled dirt, everyone knowing both where the dirt came from and to where it would be returned. I suggested to Mom, and she agreed, that it would be unnecessary, even offensive, to camouflage the dirt around Dad's grave. We asked the funeral director to instruct the cemetery personnel to leave the dirt around the grave exposed, and to provide for the lowering of the coffin into the ground while the family was present.

How could it have been otherwise? Dad's unfettered view of life revealed itself in his occasional comment when anticipating his own death. "Just wrap me in a sheet," he would say. This was not said out of lack of respect for the body, but rather from a view of life that transcended the body.

As for the grave's dirt in particular, Dad was a man for whom the earth was friend. He dug in it, planted in it, cultivated it, harvested from it, smelled it, and loved it. We would not now deny that it was earth receiving what the apostle called "the earthly tent we live in" (2 Cor. 5:1 NRSV). Instead, we would do what was simplest and most honest. There was no doubt that Dad would have approved.

Not hiding the reality of that graveside moment also served as symbolism of the person Dad had been. In Chandler Carlson you got what you saw. There was utterly no artificiality, no pretense with him. Whether in his work at the hospital or in retirement during visits in hospitals and in homes or in casual conversations on the street, and not least in importance at home as husband and father, Dad was consistently unassuming, humble, and thankful.

How were these characteristics demonstrated? When in my late teenage years, I was active in a Saturday evening church-based youth group, the same group earlier referenced that once owed a debt to a local radio station. Often, by the time I would leave home for the meeting, Dad would have polished my shoes. Yes, I hesitate to share that example, but there it is. And he did not do so because I would not; rather, it was his giving spirit at work. He did what I intended later to do.

It might be concluded that as an only child I indeed was, if not spoiled, at least catered to overmuch. Some thirty years later during a meeting in Boston, something about how I presented myself prompted a pastor colleague to say, "I *knew* you were an only child." Really? How did she know? Feminine instinct? How could my not having siblings possibly be conveyed in the course of one brief meeting? And her comment was made at midmeeting! Whatever the answer, I had long since been polishing my own shoes.

Again, Dad was consistently unassuming, humble, and thankful, the latter being expressed in his handwritten note, one written on behalf of both Mom and himself and that, as I recall, was left in our New Britain home upon their departure at the end of a visit. It is dated May 31, 1973, and reads:

Dear Ones,

Words cannot express what we want to say to you all for the good times we have had with you while here in your lovely home and church, and for including us in everything. We love you all very much. May God's richest blessings be yours in health and happiness. Mom and Dad

P.S. We will be looking forward to seeing you in August.

A Christian's perspective encourages the anticipation of being with loved ones again, be the "again" a certain month of the year or the other side of death. When the time comes, my cremated remains will be sprinkled into the earth at a New England site, one that for decades has been special to our family. Be it my father's return to the earth or my own,[36] the faith that he and Mom passed on to me transcends both depth of interment and fierceness of flame.

CHAPTER 33

---·❖·---

A Startling Revelation

A very beautiful day with sunshine. I dug some more parsnips.
Ruby and I sold our house today.
—from Dad's diary, February 14, 1974

The exact date has been forgotten, but it occurred in the mid-1980s during one of my visits home to see for myself how my parents were doing. Dad and I were alone in the living room, my mother momentarily being absent. From out of nowhere, it seemed, Dad shared the amount of interest they had received the preceding month, a subject I'd never before heard him mention. And he stated it in an uncharacteristically satisfied tone. I chose not to press him on a matter that was not my business, which is not to say that I didn't wonder about the details. They were, in fact, startling words that he had spoken, not least of all in the amount of interest itself.

In the months prior to their moving into an apartment on the LSS campus in 1974, their house on Willow Avenue had sold for $16,500—an amount when offered prompted a brother of Dad's to advise, "I'd take it and run." Ten to fifteen years later, the same house in the greater Boston area would have sold for upward of ten to fifteen times that amount.

How, then, given my parents' history, had an unusual amount of interest been earned the preceding month? Was it from one instrument alone, or did the figure Dad shared represent interest from several sources?

When my father retired, the monthly income available to him and Mom was almost what it had been when he was working 108 hours every thirteen days, i.e., forty-eight and sixty hours seriatim. The income from Social Security, plus Dad's New York State pension, resulted in that reality. Early into their marriage, in spite of initial doubt on my mother's part about how she, in her words, "could possibly squeeze one more nickel" out of Dad's meager weekly income but knowing they could opt out of the state's plan up to a certain cut-off date, they chose to give it a try. And in 1966 how thankful they were to have made that decision.

Thus, for as little as the sale of the house provided them by today's standards, they invested in a product, likely an annuity, sold by what was then Lutheran Brotherhood Insurance, a fraternal life insurance company located in Minneapolis, Minnesota. Mom had shared with me that the local agent had posted an ad for a certain product in the local newspaper to which they had responded.

Between that action and Mom's consistent and careful management of their finances, when Dad was hospitalized in December of 1986 she informed me of their financial situation. At that point in time, the assets to which they had access totaled $110,000—for them an unthinkable amount just a few years earlier. No wonder Dad had announced the interest gain with such satisfaction!

Also brought to mind is the aforementioned observation about Dad's spirit of generosity. I recall in the mid-1980s during a visit home having overheard Dad say to Mom of their then current assets, "Dan could use a little of that." The context was their knowledge of the projected cost of a house that Faith and I were having built for our retirement years. I suspect that Mom pretended not to have heard Dad's suggestion.

And indeed, reality was soon to make itself known. When in January of 1987 Dad was moved from the hospital to the Hultquist Infirmary on the LSS campus and Mom met with the CEO, Mr. Norman Berg, the latter's verbal notice to her was: "There was a time, Ruby, when $100,000 was a lot of money, but it isn't anymore." I can still hear her saying to an acquaintance as the move to the nursing home was anticipated, "It's going to take all we have!"

When Dad died in August 1989, Mom had paid his nursing home expenses. Then, by early 1997, records show that Mom's assets totaled a bit in excess of $117,000. Again, a surprising total given the expenses for Dad's care a few years earlier. Consider, too, the contrast between that figure and Mom's accounting in a modest ledger she kept beginning in 1936. The figures she recorded for all of 1938—the first full year of my parents' life in marriage and of my birth—show a total of $970.45 income, $961.40 disbursements, and a reserve of $9.05. Fifty-nine years later the Lutheran Brotherhood component was both major and essential: between an annuity, an income fund, and a municipal bond fund, Mom's immediate financial situation was secure.

During the final four years of her earthly journey, Mom was first in assisted living, then in skilled nursing care. During those years, years that included her transition into Alzheimer's disease, her decades-old, antiquelike slant-front maple desk was one of the few personal artifacts in her room. A bit earlier but as late in her life as 1994, at age eighty-six and in as short a period as five days that October, her diary reveals: on the 17th, "spent the afternoon at my desk"; on the 19th, "I worked at my desk all day"; and on the 21st, "worked at my desk." And now, her awareness slowly fading, she would sit at that desk apparently for long enough periods of time for one of the nurses to have commented to me, "We're not sure what she's doing, but there she sits." Might it not have had something to do with still, deep in her consciousness, the recognition that it was while seated at that piece of furniture that she managed the family's finances and, in a very real sense, our well-being? In those very last years, Mom wasn't so much *doing* anything as being *drawn* by the familiar.

And yet, for all of her success in her faithfully consistent stewardship of the family's financial resources beginning in 1937, by the time of her death in August of 2002, Mom had been on Medicaid for some time. Mr. Berg had been correct.

True to my parents' practice from the beginning of their marriage, Mom continued to tithe the fifty dollars that Medicaid permitted her to keep each month from the income that otherwise went to the nursing home. By then, I had been in charge of her finances for several years, each month writing the five dollar check for the church.

In the end, another verse beautifully describes in terms of human relationships what for Dad, and for Mom too, provided the most substance, the most satisfaction, the most stability and joy in life.

RICH
is not how much you have or where you are going
or even what you are
rich is who you have beside you.[37]

CHAPTER 34

Where Today?

Writing on the subject of social morality, the late C. S. Lewis offers the following that remains pertinent not least of all in the context of the growing political divisions among a people not a few of whom regard ours to be a Christian nation. Says Lewis of any potential for a Christian society:

> Most of us are not really approaching the subject in order to find out what Christianity says: we are approaching it in the hope of finding support from Christianity for the views of our own party. We are looking for an ally where we are offered either a Master or—a Judge. ... And that is why nothing whatever is going to come of such talks unless we go a much longer way round. A Christian society is not going to arrive until most of us really want it: and we are not going to want it until we become fully Christian. I may repeat "Do as you would be done by" till I am black in the face, but I cannot really carry it out till I love my neighbour as myself: and I cannot learn to

love my neighbor as myself till I learn to love God: and I cannot learn to love God except by learning to obey Him. And so, as I warned you, we are driven on to something more inward—driven on from social matters to religious matters. For the longest way round is the shortest way home.[38]

The question posed in the title above is not related to *place*, as in a person's ultimate destination. That question is entirely to be answered by my father's Creator. Rather, and more specifically, where in his thoughts, in his feelings, in his conclusions would Dad be today on the questions of immigration, national identity, and how a nation responds to people of nations adjacent or even fairly close to their own borders. As these words are written, simultaneously in the news are the issues of Israel and its Palestinian neighbors and, closer to home, of this nation's handling of the thousands of children and youth currently crossing our southwestern border.

Indeed, as these events developed my bishop in New England, the Rev. James E. Hazelwood, dedicated a blog piece addressing these two issues, the New England Synod of the Evangelical Lutheran Church in America having companion relationships both with the Evangelical Lutheran Church in Jordan and the Holy Land and with Lutherans and Episcopalians in Honduras. And his concern was echoed by Paul Brandeis Raushenbush, who wrote on July 17, 2014, in response to the events just that day from Gaza to the Ukraine: "But we are not impotent, and this is not 'happening to us.' We, the human race, are doing this to ourselves. These aren't natural disasters, or 'acts of God.' It's just us, humans, having completely lost our humanity. We are warring, and hurting, and intentionally or unintentionally killing one another through direct assault or indifference and neglect."[39]

How in the world does my father, who would be one hundred eighteen years old if he were living today, relate to such matters?

Actually, in several ways. (1) He was but one generation removed from himself having been an immigrant. (2) When I was a teenager, neighborhood family surnames included Cheetham, Dombrowski, Flanagan, and Russo, reminders enough of the immigrant mixture around us. And (3), at work Dad related to a number of individuals of Italian background, that having been second to the Swedish presence and influence in Jamestown. I say influence, remembering once being in a barber shop at election time and overhearing a conversation that centered on local politics. The barber himself was a second- or third-generation American of Italian descent. Several men were discussing the approaching election, local candidates, and possible election results when one voice offered the observation that "the Swedish lodges in this town have everything all tied up anyway."

On much another level of influence, occasionally during our Charles Street years in the 1940s, our little family would stop in at an ice-cream parlor at the eastern end of the Third Street bridge. Our consistently favorite sundae? The Mexican sundae. Were we unknowingly and literally enjoying a taste of what was to come several decades into the future?

My dad paid attention to the news both on radio and on television. When in his later years his diary notes that he'd taken time to read, the newspaper was likely a primary focus. I recall that, at some point in the decades-long Israeli-Arab hostilities, he spoke briefly but negatively of the Arab parties to the conflict. In doing so, he used the word *Arab* rather than *Palestinian* in his comment.

Sometime later when I shared Dad's comment with his grandson, Curtis, the latter expressed disappointment. "I'm sorry to hear that," he said. Each of Dad's grandchildren demonstrate open and generous attitudes toward sharers of the human experience whatever their national origin, background, language, or color. Carolyn, in her work as a retail sales manager, having been in both Illinois and North Carolina before her present location in Colorado, comes in contact with a variety of individuals, whether customers or fellow employees. Curtis, as a family nurse practitioner in Down East Maine, speaks

Spanish when responding to the needs especially of migrant farm workers.

I am certain that Dad, when in the single instance here related implied empathy for the Jewish state and not for its Arab, and especially Palestinian, neighbors, was reflecting, to use Lewis' term, chiefly a party view compared to one based on a personal and intentional less than egalitarian evaluation of the neighbors' mutual interests. Also to be taken into account is Dad's awareness of the inextricable connection historically between the Hebrew and Christian stories.

Where would Dad be today in his view of contemporary, daily, and global illustrations of humankind's gross failures to live those purposes the Creator intends? He would be the first to admit his own imperfections, i.e., his own culpability in the human self-created dilemma. At least in his lifetime, the church's worship began with the corporate admission of same. And in today's increasingly sharp and unyielding lines of political give and take, he would be as susceptible as anyone to being persuaded by one side as against another. I have little doubt, too, that he would recognize the validity of the judgment that "every decision requires forgiveness"—a quote the source of which I do not recall.

If Lewis were writing today, one wonders what influence the current emphasis on, indeed, reality of, pluralism would have on his vision of the road leading to a Christian society. Specifically, what impact might the increasing presence both of Islam and, ironically, of a seemingly more vocal atheism in Western culture have on his prescription? Might his "longest way round" by now be even longer?

All of which still leaves, in my view, the man, the father, my dad as portrayed in the preceding chapters, an essentially caring, giving, accepting person, one who prayed for foe as well as for friend.

CHAPTER 35

His Gift

Pray with confidence;
Serve with joy;
Work with zeal;
Live with gratitude.[40]

The stock market crash of 1929, the event that for many was so defining, occurred when Dad was thirty-two years old. It was still eight years until he would marry, and he wasn't yet working full time at the hospital. As a boy in the 1940s and 1950s, I heard the occasional story of the Great Depression in family conversations, but such stories were few and far between and hardly ever about the immediate family. Grandpa Haskell was a fireman, working for the city. His pay was modest but regular. Grandpa Carlson and his sheet metal business always had work throughout the 1930s because, as Dad said, "The work was done well and the prices were fair." In other words, there were no family stories, at least none that I heard, about children going hungry or not having enough to wear.

I share that background in acknowledging my awareness that these recollections of my father are written from a middle-class perspective and from a particular one that was not formed as drastically by the 1930s crucible as were the histories of so many families. Today, as our culture begins to show signs of ever more widening gaps between income groups—not to mention the most recent dramatic economic downturn, that of 2008 and following—it would be understandable were the objection raised that the illustrations in the preceding chapters of having little are flawed; that any suggestion of being in lack when in fact one has enough, even if it is *just* enough, is itself lacking.

Equally compelling is to acknowledge that the everyday cost of living was lower during the time here being considered. And yes, our family was as present as any other family in the age of acquisition, the years of which began soon after the end of World War II. Yet my mother didn't buy what she referred to as housedresses at one of the local five-and-dime stores simply to appear humble. The necessity of household budget adjustments, allowing for considerably more public transportation usage in getting Dad both to and from work after the move from Charles Street to Willow Avenue—that necessity was real. And except for a few outside work clothes that hung in the basement, during all of my years before departing for college, one modestly sized closet—*one*—held all of Mom's, Dad's, and my hanging clothes, some of them, of course, for dress up only. Compared to the size of walk-in closets in many of today's recently built houses—some providing more space than the tents of the homeless—the space required for the three of us, at just over a clothes hanger's capacity in width and about ten feet in length, was minimal.

Dad's claim, however, was never that he had enough. His claim was that he had *everything*. Whenever he would hear of someone else having good fortune—a new car, a job promotion, a trip to some far-off place—his response more often than not was, "More power to them!" If he secretly wished for similar opportunities, he kept that to himself. Yet, since for most of us such longings are not easy to hide, I believe that Dad's expressions of contentment were genuine.

Indeed, as a father of a bride said to me a few years ago, the principal ingredient in a marriage that lasts is precisely that—contentment.

At the base of his overriding satisfaction with life was a simple but deep spirituality, indeed, faith. My Aunt Adeline says of Dad regarding his encounter with the Swedish Salvation Army evangelist from whom came the inspiration to discard the pocketed cigar butt, "What a change!" That faith, in turn, engendered a sense of gratitude that was a centering force for the duration of his life. Without ever being aware of what would come to be modern parlance, my father was centered.

It was that centeredness, I believe, that so endeared Dad to those who knew him, not least of all those who knew him in the sphere of his work. Although in that setting, deeds combined with words, giving their lasting impression. Did his words have the deeper impact? Probably in all those years working in the hospital, no patient ever heard more than a gentle "God bless you" upon Dad's departure from a bedside. Yet it is also probable that more patients than not sensed something of the deep well from whence that assuring palliative came.

Contemporary physician and writer Dr. Andrew Weil has said of today's medical doctors that "(they) are not very well trained in the authority and power that their words have in the healing process."[41] It is unlikely that many of the testimonies Dad heard in his lifetime to the effectiveness of his presence in caring for the ill drew a distinction between words and deeds. And I am not at all certain of the extent to which he himself was aware that his words were equal in power to his deeds. I do believe he understood that, in his work especially, he was effecting what is anticipated in a contemporary Prayer after Communion: "Enliven us by your presence in this meal, that we may be your presence in the world."

For the record and by my mother's account, Dad's 1987 transition into the LSS nursing home was the occasion for a rare vocal self-acknowledgement of his vocational contribution to the community. Shortly into his stay as a resident there, he was told where he was to be more permanently placed. It was to be in a unit that housed residents far less cognizant of reality than he was. His response to that news was almost startling: "After *all I've done* for this place?" He referred not least of all, I'm sure, to his activity level among residents in all the time following his retirement twenty-one years earlier. And the result of his plaintive question? He was placed in a unit suitable for someone still having his keen level of awareness, his words clearly having been effective.

In what was the Jamestown General Hospital, there hangs a plaque here shown:

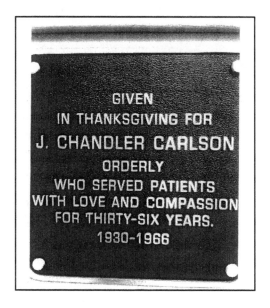

Remembering my father helps me keep my sense of perspective in a time and a culture where, in spite of current economic stresses, the balance between being grateful and "having it better than one's father had it" remains heavily weighted, and too often grossly distorted, by acquisition's fever. And in whatever ways my life reflects the goodness of the man I knew as Dad, the example he has left in both word and deed is his gift.

CHAPTER 36

———◆———

Ringing ~ Silently

In the late winter-early spring of 1955, I purchased a ring with the assistance of jeweler Earl Griffith of Griffith's Jewelry on West Third Street, Jamestown. The ring's stone was red, as in synthetic ruby red, and at my request Mr. Griffith, a member of our church, saw to a gold cross being encrusted into the stone's center.

Although the ring cost then, in contrast to what it might cost in today's economy, a mere forty-five dollars, I'm sure it was paid for in installments, as at the time when a sophomore in high school I earned seven dollars weekly working on Saturdays for a local restaurant equipment supply company. My job was to clean the store—sweeping floors, dusting shelves, cleaning the restroom, washing windows and, at day's end, the owners' cars as well. Never having washed a car before, hardly ever did I get that quite right, and either Tony or John Valone, and sometimes both, would just look at their vehicles, shake their heads, and walk away. Still, they treated me well, and I enjoyed working for them. Years later they, both Roman Catholics, attended an event in town at which I'd been invited to speak—interestingly, an event held at a Salvation Army location—after Faith and I had been to a historic ecumenical event at St. Peter's Basilica in Rome.

At the conclusion of my shift on April 9, Holy Saturday, I realized that the ring was missing. So choice was I of its newness and not wanting to mar it as I went about my cleaning chores, I would remove the ring, slipping it into my pocket under my coveralls. On this day, the ring had not fallen into the intended pocket.

The ring was not a gift, nor had it been at my parents' expense. Yet I hesitated to tell them of the loss, as that was attributable to my own carelessness. It wasn't until Monday the 18th that, before leaving home for school, I attached a note to the laundry that Mom would be tending later in the day.

Mom's response was first to call another jewelry store in town, one known also to be a pawn shop. They had no knowledge of the ring, but having been advised to call the police, Mom followed through. What she learned from the officer when on the telephone was both startling and shocking.

On the day I had lost the ring, a man had gone to the police with a ring he had found, first having approached a priest, thinking the cross-bearing artifact might be his. When it turned out not to be the priest's, the finder went to the police, wondering whether the ring might have been reported as stolen.

What the officer then said to Mom was the following: two days after going to the police, the man took his own life while at home. That was on Easter Monday. Meanwhile, of course, burial had occurred. Was the ring possibly even now with the deceased?

The only recourse was to contact the grieving widow, and that my mother did. Not having overheard her side of the conversation, I am certain that she was sensitive and caring as she introduced herself, approaching, in measured steps, what was prompting the call. Finally, the deceased's widow asked that the ring be described, and upon hearing the description she said, "I have your ring."

The couple resided within easy walking distance from Washington Street, the location of my Saturday employment, a street that I traversed four times each Saturday both coming to and going from work, and also a similar trek during the lunch hour. There is little doubt but that the ring had been dropped from my hand, not into a pocket, but instead into a trouser cuff and from there onto the sidewalk or street. Its journey after being dislodged from my clothing and into the eyesight, then hands, of the gentleman I neither knew nor would ever meet continues to beg the question: What possible influence, if any, might the ring itself have had on the man during his final hours from Holy Saturday, through Easter Day, and into Easter Monday? It's a haunting question.

My mother's role in this story is obvious. She served as the one-person search party. But my father's role? Less than a decade later Paul Simon's song, "The Sound of Silence," itself somewhat haunting, became popular. While Dad was privy to all of the detail of this lost and found drama, what he said aloud, both in quantity and with fervor, probably did not match what was expressed within himself—his silent spirit hoping, then rejoicing, indeed veritably ringing his thanks at the outcome *and* praying on behalf of the deceased man and his family.

Earlier chapters have addressed both my mom's first love and the manner in which her voice often spoke in contrast to Dad's relative quietness. Upon Matthew Hoff's death, his father, according to Mom's legacy notes, "said I was too good for this world and I should go to a convent." Given the relative quietness associated with life in a convent, the irony of the father's judgment is perhaps obvious, not least of all in the episode here related—Mom's voice having been the instrument through which the lost was found.

As for my dad, the quieter of the two, his role I value as much; for no less was he himself an instrument. Yes, ringing, although silently. And, to this day, I wear the ring.[42]

CHAPTER 37

---•◆•---

Dreams Fulfilled

You are never too old to set another goal or to
dream a new dream.[43]—C. S. Lewis

It was Thanksgiving Day 2013. We were already present, my wife and I, at the home of friends, when relatives of theirs, a nephew and his wife, arrived on the scene. When another dinner guest asked the nephew, "How's it going?" he responded, "I'm living a dream!" And his was not a detached response; he answered with enthusiasm.

The nephew's verbal expression was fairly new to me. Perhaps at my age I'm simply not current with the latest phrases of common usage. But I understood his response to be positive. After all, dreams are of varied content. The nephew might have said, "I'm living a nightmare!"

Dreams of the while-sleeping variety are a common experience with me. In terms of recognizing characters who share my dreams, that is a mixture. Some I recognize, others I don't. The closest to a nightmare with all of its stress and tension usually has centered on my work in the church, specifically in the context of a congregation and its worship. I once dreamt that a number of distractions were delaying my entrance into the church nave for the beginning of the liturgy. I realized what was happening, felt the stress and tension, but was ineffective in doing anything about it. The result? When at last I did enter the nave to greet the people, no one was there. It was a large and empty space; everyone had departed. I was both not surprised and yet stunned.

Regarding that nightmare as described, and given his *The Future of an Illusion*, I wonder what Freud's interpretation would be? And would I really want to know? But Freud notwithstanding, dreams have their place in holy Scripture. Consider:

> In Genesis 37, the writer says, "Once Joseph had a dream, and when he told it to his brothers, they hated him even more" (v. 5 NRSV). Joseph's dream foretold what was yet to occur in their relationship, an incident reviewed in a preceding chapter.

> In Matthew 2, the writer says of the wise men's visit to Mary's infant child, "Then, opening their treasure chests, they offered him gifts of gold, frankincense, and myrrh. And having been warned in a dream not to return to Herod, they left for their own country by another road" (vv. 11b–12 NRSV). Singer-songwriter James Taylor has a thought-provoking song based on verse 12, one titled "Home by Another Way."[44] Verse 13 tells of Joseph's dream in which an angel instructs him to "take the child and his mother, and flee to Egypt, and remain there until I tell you; for Herod is about to search for the child, to destroy him."

> And in Acts 2 the writer, referencing the prophet Joel, says: "In the last days it will be, God declares, that I will pour out my Spirit upon all flesh, and your sons and your daughters shall prophesy, and your young

men shall see visions, and your old men shall dream
dreams" (v. 17 NRSV).

Clearly, dreams are not just the result of contemporary stresses
and strains on the conscious and subconscious—not that either is
impervious to such influences. But rather, dreams and their influence
have been around a long time, as have the stresses and strains that
affect human existence.

How all of this relates to my father is to a large degree guesswork.
I don't recall discussing dreams with Dad or with Mom either for that
matter. Not that I didn't have such a conversation with either one of
them, but I simply don't recall. At the same time, the sense in which
C. S. Lewis uses the term very much relates to both of my parents,
and not least of all to Dad.

Lewis' statement above, and especially given the presence of *goal*
also in the statement, includes *dream*, I believe, in the sense of "a
strongly desired goal or purpose."[45] Thus, whether in his younger
years or older, what can one reasonably think of Dad having strongly
desired in either goal or purpose? Or, in other words and in that sense,
what were my father's dreams?

No doubt my mother's name would appear at the top of the
list, the dream having been—however he might have articulated it
internally and however delayed in his life the dream materialized—to
live a fulfilling life, one that included marriage.

Next would appear my name and those of my wife and of our two
children, the names appearing in the chronological order of when
each individual came into his life. Although Dad died eight years
before his first great-grandchild was born, for the four of us who
were part of his life, he would have given thanks and dreamed of a
purposeful life for each of us.

Dad's work at the hospital having been a dominating force from
1930–1966, his dream of good health for himself and for those he
loved had to have been a constant and, not least of all, that he would
be healthy during his retirement years.

As for both goals and purpose, each is amply addressed and summarized in Dad's annual planning for, then carrying out those plans, in his love of vegetable gardening, especially in his retirement, never-too-old years! Note in Epilogue II that follows his granddaughter's mention of how he expanded the assigned personal planting space in what, in fact, was a shared planting area overall— expanded it to a nearby area claimed by no one else.

Finally, who knows how both goal and purpose were crucial to the healing process during his relatively youthful hospitalization of 1917–1918? And while his return home was several weeks prior to the beginning of Advent, the season that anticipates the "good news of great joy" (Luke 2:10 NRSV), how could he not joyfully have been anticipating that return?

My eternal thanks that the healing happened, that Dad returned home, that eventually, with my mother, a new home was established, one into which I would be born. Only because of that ordinary, indeed commonplace yet dreamlike sequence, have these words been written. Ordinary—commonplace. How very fitting, given the uncomplicated and accessible person my father was, a person so well described by the apostle's words to the Colossians:

"Clothe yourselves with compassion, kindness, humility, meekness, and patience. Bear with one another and, if anyone has a complaint against another, forgive each other; just as the Lord has forgiven you, so you also must forgive. Above all, clothe yourselves with love, which binds everything together in perfect harmony ... And be thankful" (Col. 3:12–15 NRSV).

Epilogue I

The previous chapter briefly mentioned the great-grandchildren my father never met. How very much he would have loved and enjoyed both Seamus, now seventeen years old, and Jacob, now fourteen. The boys, living near the coast in Down East Maine, are accustomed to being in their dad's boat and tending the several lobster traps for which they are licensed. Also having a pond near their house, they are very familiar with the water.

Dad's family of origin, although having a cottage on the shores of Chautauqua Lake, to my knowledge was not much an on-the-water group of individuals. However, from everything above that has preceded these words, it is not difficult to imagine how much Dad, and Mom in equal measure, would have appreciated the story that follows. Written in the summer of 2005 when Faith and I still had our fourteen-foot Phantom sailboat and our grandsons had been with us for a few days at Camp Calumet Lutheran in Freedom, New Hampshire, the brief piece first appeared in that August's edition of *Calumet Alumni News*. As both the writer and the relatively inept sailor, to this day the experience remains fresh in my memory.

Seamus, Jacob ~ ~ ~ and Jesus

Late morning on Monday, July 11, I took our eight-year-old grandson, Seamus, out for a ride in our Phantom sailboat. Later in the day, Hayden Anderson would share with me that he could tell just by reading the water (my phrase) that, as he said, "We'd be having trouble out there today."

However, not reading the water, out went Seamus and I, only to discover that it was extremely difficult to set a course for any length of time due to the gusty and erratic winds. After making it clear for about the fifth time that he would just as soon be back on shore, a gust of wind treated Seamus to the sight of his grandpa slipping off the boat backward into the water. Because I was entangled in both rope and a life jacket, it took at least fifteen minutes to extricate myself from each, thus enabling me, although still with considerable effort, to get back into the boat. Meanwhile, our family on the beach (including staff-nurse alum Faith and staff alum Carolyn, '80s) had enlisted the help of pontoon boat pilot John, and soon we were mercifully towed in to shore.

On Tuesday the 12th, our son, Curtis (he, too, a staff alum from the '80s), took our youngest grandson, Jacob, for a sail. The winds being cooperative, they had a pleasant time, during which the four-year-old said, "Papa, I'm glad you're sailing the boat instead of Grandpa because you stay in the boat." Happily, I took the boat out again, alone, two more times during the week and, especially on Saturday the 16th, enjoyed a wonderful sail with strong and consistent winds moving boat and rider back and forth across beautiful Ossipee Lake.

I have long felt that sailing is so very stimulating in part because the sound of the boat moving through the water is exactly a sound with which Jesus himself was familiar. No motor's noise and none of the motor's odors. Instead, just the wind and the sail and the slapping, splashing, and rippling sounds of the water, as nature and fabric move boat and passenger along. It's a great sensation, especially when the winds are harmonious with the sailor's intentions. But even when they aren't, what an assuring article of faith it is that on the water, as in all of life and regardless of the conditions, Jesus is with us!

———•———

By 2005 both of my parents had died. But had they together ever had the opportunity to become aware of that brief story, I believe they would have smiled, of course also sharing a comment or two, perhaps even shedding a few tears while, at the same time, being thankful—thankful for such a witness to the faith journey, the journey on which the Calmer of the Sea is known still to be present (Matt. 8:23–27 NRSV).

Epilogue II

Carolyn Faith Carlson

The last time I saw my grandpa was exactly one week before he died. I believe that, other than my grandma and the nurses who cared for him, I was his last visitor. I know I was his last visitor from out-of-town.

When I saw him that day, he was frail, blind, and could hardly hear. Even when I yelled into his ear, he didn't know who I was. I felt I should leave but was torn. Since I knew he didn't know I was there, I made one more attempt to get him to recognize me. Finally, his silent world was broken. The connection was made. How could I have known that as I hugged him it would be for the last time?

I didn't know my grandpa either as a young man or as a man in his prime of life. He was seventy-three years old when I was born. I myself was only becoming aware of my own adulthood when he died. What I do know is simple.

He married when he was forty and lived to celebrate his and my grandma's fiftieth wedding anniversary. He was a very kind man, the gentlest man I have ever known. He loved gardening, and every year, even when walking had become difficult, he would expand the area planted by claiming other pieces of land that his peers were either unable or chose not to tend. He had a pack of Juicy Fruit gum every time I visited and always gave me a stick. He was a member of The Clean Plate Club, never failing to eat everything on his plate, which is why, I tell myself, I clean mine. He played Yahtzee with Grandma every Sunday night at the dining room table, the cuckoo clock slowly ticking away the hours. Often after dinner he fell asleep, his white-haired head falling backward onto the headrest of his favorite antique rocking chair. He loved his family. At his memorial service, he was spoken of time and again as a saint and as the most generous, faithful man anyone knew.

I remember him as my grandpa.

Afterword

Two Memorable Statements
and
One Pressing Question

~ *from the distant past* ~
"We are treated ... as having nothing,
and yet
possessing everything" (2 Cor. 6:8b, 10c NRSV).

~ *from the recent past* ~
"I am grateful for what I am and have.
My thanksgiving is perpetual.
It is surprising how contented one can be
with nothing definite—only a sense of existence."[46]

~ *in the present* ~
"How are we of material privilege to act in our day
to assure that there is the possibility
of an inhabitable planet for future generations, i.e.,
for *both* the human *and* all other created species?"[47]

Endnotes

1   Dorsett, Lyle W., Editor, *The Essential C.S. Lewis*. New York: Collier Books, Macmillan Publishing Company, 1988, p. 523.

2   Atkinson, Brooks, Editor, *Walden and Other Writings of Henry David Thoreau*. New York: The Modern Library, 1992, p. 87.

3   In the early 1970s, *Newsweek* magazine, in an article on the city's newly built city hall, began by describing Jamestown as "a down-at-the-heels town on the edge of New York's western frontier." Just a few years earlier the description would have been very different. The Jamestown of the 1940s and 1950s was a bustling industrial city, the home of several widely known manufacturers, including Crescent Tool, Art Metal, Blackstone Corp., Dahlstrom Metallic Door, Hope's Windows, Inc., and also many fine furniture companies, among which was Jamestown Royal Upholstery. The city boasted its own furniture mart, located alongside the tracks of the Erie Railroad that ran through the center of town. In early 1965 the writer and his wife, when purchasing their first furniture, were met by a manufacturer's representative at The Merchandise Mart in Chicago. Having been advised of our budget, the representative declined to show us Jamestown Royal Upholstery items because, as he said, "They are beyond what your budget will allow."

4   The hospital is now known as the Jones Memorial Health Center, and as reported "In Years Past" by *The Post-Journal*, Jamestown, New York, August 9, 2013: "In 1988, the City of Jamestown took a major and difficult step in relieving itself of mounting deficits incurred by Jamestown General Hospital by selling the 77-year-old facility to WCA Hospital for $5 million." Today the WCA Hospital remains Jamestown's only hospital.

5   From "Think Baby Names"; via the Internet: www.thinkbabynames.com.

6   Today that absence in their daily life would be almost stylish. According to Pete Bigelow, associate editor, AOL Autos, in an Internet piece appearing

on October 6, 2013, between 1960 and 2007, no-car families decreased to an all-time low of 8.7 percent. By 2011, that percentage had increased to 9.3 percent. Contributing factors included communication substituting for travel; renewed interest in transit, biking, walking; all of which, wrote Bigelow, "helped dampen interest in expanding auto ownership."

7   As a teenager, the actress-to-be had once been in my mother's girlhood home, Lucille being in junior high school with Mom's younger sister, Gladys. Their mother advised that it would be best that her daughter not keep company with the girl. The reason: Lucille wore slacks. How very strangely that comes across today, remembering the actress as the epitome of mid-twentieth century sitcom wholesomeness, not to mention what today passes as acceptable both in dress and in on-screen behavior, be it TV or film. Note: Not only were Mom and her sister contemporaries of Lucille Ball, but also of Roger Tory Peterson, who grew up in the same neighborhood as they. 1908 was the birth year of both him and my mother.

8   From an interview at Eastern Washington University, Spokane, April 24, 2006; originally appearing in print in the June 2006 edition of *Willow Springs* 58; via the Internet: willowspringsewu@gmail.com.

9   From Snopes.com, Jimmy Carter on Helping the Poor; via the Internet.

10   Lenker, John Nicholas, Editor, *Sermons of Martin Luther*, Vol. 1. Grand Rapids: Baker Book House, 1988, p. 144.

11   Many years later, it would be Dr. Miller's grandniece who would meet and capture the heart of this author, our marriage occurring on September 5, 1964.

12   Steiner, Margarete, Translator and Compiler, *Day by Day We Magnify Thee*. Philadelphia: Fortress Press 1982, p. 32.

13   Specifics of the lake's history as reported both in *Figure 8 the Lake* by Thomas A. Erlandson and Linda V. Swanson, Eagles Publishing, Jamestown, New York, 2004, pp. 38, 39, 195; and in *Steamboat Landing*, City of Jamestown, New York, 2008; via the Internet: http://www.jamestownny.net/index.php/parks-and-recreation/historial-marker-program/steamboat-landing.

14   "The exact words are in dispute; their sentiment is not." The editors of Encyclopaedia Britannica; via the Internet: www.britannica.com.

15   *The Post-Journal*, July 29, 1950, p. 17; courtesy of Prendergast Library, Jamestown, NY.

16   *Liturgy and Spiritual Awakening*, translated by Clifford Ansgar Nelson. Rock Island: Augustana Book Concern, 1950.

17   A quote from "Birth Order/Theories," Wikipedia; via the Internet: en.m.wikipedia.org/wiki/Birth_order.

18 In a note from Dr. Iton granting the writer permission to paraphrase the address's central points, he reveals that, during his college and medical school days, he himself worked as an orderly.

19 In fact, technically Dad was a licensed practical nurse, having had his license since January 31, 1941. It was a time in New York State when one could acquire such a designation on the signature of a physician. Dad's final license is dated September 1, 1966; he was licensed by the State Education Department. How delighted he would be today to know that not only was his daughter-in-law's vocation that of a nurse (of which he was aware) but also that his grandson would one day be a family nurse practitioner. His granddaughter, a retail sales manager in a nationwide outdoor sporting equipment chain, insists that she is engaged in therapeutic work—that of retail therapy.

20 This is a portion of the article accompanied by the photograph showing my father assisting a patient into a wheelchair.

21 My father was not aware at the time, if ever he was, that Empirin products were among the thirty-six pharmaceutical products that his daughter-in-law's father, Dr. E. A. Holstius, was instrumental in developing during his thirty-one-year vocation in the industry's research and development programs.

22 Ralph Waldo Emerson, from "Brainy Quote"; via the Internet: www.brainyquote.com.

23 From Quotable Quotes, *Reader's Digest* magazine, May 2014, p. 152.

24 From an address to New England Lutherans at Sturbridge, Massachusetts, June 8, 1995; used by permission of Dr. Nestingen.

25 A quote from Jean-Anthelme Brillat-Savarin appearing in an ad for *Food: A Cultural Culinary History* by Ken Albala, in *The Nation* magazine, October 28, 2013, p. 19.

26 Yoruban proverb. *The Penguin Dictionary of Proverbs*. London: Penguin Books, 1983, p. 95.

27 Gomes, Peter J., *The Good Book*. New York: William Morrow and Company, Inc., 1996, pp. 78–80.

28 Hymn No. 742, Text: Joseph Scriven, 1820–1886. *Evangelical Lutheran Worship*. Augsburg Fortress, 2006.

29 Sittler, Joseph A., *Grace Notes and Other Fragments*. Philadelphia: Fortress Press, 1981, p. 14.

30 *Time*, September 30, 2013, an article by Harry McCracken and Lev Grossman.

31 *Time*, February 10, 2011, "2045: The Year Man Becomes Immortal." Via the Internet: content.time.com/time/magazine/article/0,9171,2048299.00. html.

32 *Time*, December 29, 2014 / January 5, 2015, an article by Ray Kurzweil, p. 28.

33 Hymn titled "This World Is Not My Home," Albert E. Bromley, copyright 1936.

34 Belcher, Jim, *In Search of Deep Faith*. Downers Grove, Illinois: InterVarsity Press, 2013, p. 242.

35 Hymn No. 793, Text: Irish 8th cent. *Evangelical Lutheran Worship*. Augsburg Fortress, 2006.

36 Genesis 3:19b. "You are dust, and to dust you shall return." *The Holy Bible*, New Revised Standard Version. Grand Rapids: Zondervan, 1989.

37 Jack I. Kohler's verse; a calligraphy print by Michael Podesta; via the Internet: www.shopatsainttmarks.org/CardsMP.html.

38 Dorsett, Lyle, W., *The Essential C.S. Lewis*. New York: Collier Books, Macmillan Publishing Company, 1988, p. 318.

39 "The Blog." The Huffington Post, July 17, 2014; via the Internet: www. huffingtonpost.com/the-blog.

40 William Arthur Ward; written source unknown.

41 From an interview with Dr. Andrew Weil, author of *Spontaneous Healing*, as heard on "Fresh Air with Terry Gross," National Public Radio, July 13, 1995. Used by permission of Terry Gross.

42 In fact, it is not the same ring I wear, i.e., not exactly. During the winter of 1964–65 it was temporarily lost a second time. My bride and I were living in Rock Island, Illinois, while I completed theological education and she began work as a surgical nurse at neighboring Moline Lutheran Hospital from which she had graduated the previous August. Having no idea what had become of the ring, one sunny winter's day on the way to the car outside of the apartment where we lived a shiny glint alongside the curb caught my attention. There, in two pieces, the stone separated from its flattened shank, lay the ring. The stone remained unsettled until late summer when we had moved to our first parish in West Warwick, Rhode Island. Then, a local jeweler, Guertin's, would reset the stone into a new shank. Thus, it's the same ring, almost.

43 From "Brainy Quote"; via the Internet: www.bainyquote.com.

44 As heard on Taylor's 1988 album, *Never Die Young*.

45 *Merriam Webster*; via the Internet: www.merriam-webster.com.

46 Henry David Thoreau, in a letter to Harrison Gray Otis Blake dated December 6, 1856, as reprinted by *Real Simple* magazine in its November 2013 issue, p. 6.

47 A question posed by the Rev. Dr. Lisa Dahill, associate professor of Worship and Christian Spirituality, Trinity Lutheran Seminary, Columbus, Ohio, when speaking in New England on October 17, 2013.

CPSIA information can be obtained at www.ICGtesting.com
Printed in the USA
BVOW07*1213250215

388947BV00001BA/3/P